A Next-Generation Tech Incubator

Paramendra Kumar Bhagat

Book Outline: *The Next-Generation Tech Incubator: Building the Future of Innovation*

Introduction: The Evolution of Investment and Innovation (Page 6)

- Overview of how tech incubators have evolved from passive investors to active ecosystem builders.
- Setting the stage for the challenges and opportunities in today's rapidly changing innovation landscape.

Part I: The Foundations of a Next-Generation Tech Incubator

Chapter 1: From Checks to Ecosystems (Page 13)

- The historical role of investors.
- Transition to active engagement with startups and the ecosystem.

Chapter 2: Building Support Systems That Thrive (Page 20)

- Designing robust support systems, including marketing and operational teams.
- Case studies of successful incubators that excel in competitive markets.

Chapter 3: Co-Investing for Success (Page 27)

- The importance of collaborative investment strategies.
- How partnerships within the ecosystem amplify startup success.

Part II: Tackling the Challenge of Exponential Innovation

Chapter 4: The Steepening Curve of Innovation (Page 36)

- Exploring the acceleration of technological innovation over the past 20 years.
- Analysis of "Internet-scale" technologies and their convergence.

Chapter 5: The Complexity of Predicting the Future (Page 43)

- Challenges in forecasting the impact of intersecting technologies.
- Frameworks for navigating uncertainty in innovation.

Chapter 6: The Problem-Solving Lens (Page 51)

- Shifting focus from technology-driven to problem-driven innovation.
- How addressing real-world challenges creates resilience against market shifts.

Part III: Tools, Trends, and Transformation

Chapter 7: The Role of Tools in Problem-Solving (Page 60)

- Differentiating between tool-builders and problem-solvers.
- Case study: Dropbox vs. industry giants like Amazon and Google.

Chapter 8: Governments as Clients and Partners (Page 68)

- Opportunities for tech startups to address large-scale problems for governments.

- Examples of successful public-private partnerships in tech innovation.

Chapter 9: Innovation Beyond Technology (Page 77)

- Exploring advancements in group dynamics, collaboration, and organizational models.
- How social innovation supports technological breakthroughs.

Part IV: The Future of Next-Generation Incubators

Chapter 10: Rethinking Metrics of Success (Page 86)

- Moving beyond financial ROI to include impact on society and the environment.
- New metrics for evaluating startup success.

Chapter 11: Building for Sustainability (Page 94)

- How incubators can ensure long-term relevance in a rapidly changing world.
- Embracing adaptability and continuous learning.

Chapter 12: The Vision Ahead (Page 102)

- Imagining the next evolution of tech incubators.
- Inspiring a generation of investors, entrepreneurs, and innovators to solve the world's biggest problems.

Conclusion: Innovating for a Better Tomorrow (Page 110)

- Recap of the principles of a next-generation tech incubator.

- Call to action for stakeholders in the innovation ecosystem to rise to the challenge.

The Evolution of Investment and Innovation

Over the last few decades, the role of investors in the startup ecosystem has undergone a profound transformation. In the past, the typical investor relationship with startups was relatively straightforward and transactional: write a check, attend board meetings, and provide periodic advice. While these actions formed the foundation for many successful ventures, they also highlighted a gap in the ecosystem. Many startups faltered not due to a lack of funding but because they lacked the comprehensive support systems necessary to navigate the complex journey from ideation to scalable success. This realization has spurred the rise of a new paradigm in investment: the next-generation tech incubator.

Today, next-generation tech incubators represent a pivotal shift in how innovation is nurtured. They go beyond simply providing funding—they actively engage with startups, offering not just capital but also resources, mentorship, and an expansive network of relationships within the ecosystem. This approach acknowledges that while money is essential, it is only one part of the equation. Startups thrive when they are embedded in an environment designed to address their challenges at every stage of growth, from product development to market entry and beyond.

From Passive to Active Investment

In the early days of venture capitalism, the investor's role was largely passive. Investors provided funding and occasionally participated in strategic decision-making during board meetings. While this model worked for some companies, it left many startups to fend for themselves in areas where they lacked expertise, such as marketing, operations, and scaling. This hands-off approach often limited the potential of otherwise promising ventures.

The dot-com boom of the late 1990s and early 2000s marked a turning point. As the pace of technological advancement accelerated, investors began to recognize that they needed to offer more than just financial support. The internet revolution created a tidal wave of new opportunities but also introduced unprecedented levels of competition and complexity. This environment demanded a more hands-on approach, one that involved not just funding but also guidance and strategic support.

Next-generation tech incubators emerged in response to this need. These incubators are not just investors; they are active partners. They engage deeply with startups, helping them navigate challenges and seize opportunities. By providing access to mentorship, market insights, and operational expertise, incubators have redefined what it means to support a startup. They have become integral to the success of many of today's most innovative companies.

The Power of Ecosystem Relationships

One of the defining characteristics of next-generation tech incubators is their emphasis on ecosystem relationships. Startups do not exist in isolation; they are part of a broader network that includes other startups, investors, corporations, academic institutions, and government entities. By cultivating extensive relationships within this ecosystem, incubators create a supportive environment that fosters collaboration and innovation.

For example, an incubator might connect a startup with potential co-investors, enabling it to secure the funding needed to scale. It might also introduce the startup to strategic partners who can help with product development or market entry. These connections are often as valuable as the initial funding itself, if not more so. They provide startups with access to resources, expertise, and markets that would otherwise be out of reach.

In addition to fostering external relationships, incubators also build internal communities. Startups within an incubator often collaborate and learn from one another, sharing insights and experiences. This sense of community is particularly important in the early stages of a startup's journey, when founders are navigating uncharted territory and facing significant uncertainty. By creating a collaborative environment, incubators help startups build the resilience and adaptability needed to succeed.

Support Systems That Thrive

The competitive nature of today's markets demands more robust support systems than ever before. Next-generation tech incubators recognize this and have built support structures designed to thrive in dynamic, high-pressure environments. These support systems often include specialized teams that provide expertise in key areas such as marketing, product development, legal compliance, and customer acquisition.

For instance, a marketing team within an incubator might help a startup refine its value proposition, craft a compelling brand narrative, and execute targeted campaigns. This level of support goes far beyond traditional investor involvement and reflects a deeper understanding of what startups need to succeed in today's competitive landscape.

Moreover, these support systems are not static; they evolve alongside the startups they serve. As a startup grows and its needs change, the incubator adapts its support to meet those needs. This dynamic approach ensures that startups receive the right support at the right time, maximizing their chances of success.

The Challenge of Identifying Promising Startups

While providing funding and support is essential, the true test of a next-generation tech incubator lies in its ability to identify promising startups in an era of rapid technological change. The pace of innovation has accelerated dramatically in recent years, creating both opportunities and challenges for investors.

The rise of exponential technologies—such as artificial intelligence, blockchain, quantum computing, and biotech—has made it increasingly difficult to predict which startups will succeed. These technologies are evolving at a breakneck pace, and their intersections create new possibilities that are often impossible to foresee. For example, the convergence of AI and biotech has given rise to groundbreaking advancements in personalized medicine, while the integration of blockchain and IoT is transforming supply chain management.

In this environment, traditional methods of evaluating startups are no longer sufficient. Investors must adopt new frameworks that account for the complexity and uncertainty of the innovation landscape. This often involves looking beyond the technology itself and focusing on the real-world problems that a startup is trying to solve.

A Problem-Solving Lens

One of the most effective ways to navigate the complexity of today's innovation landscape is to adopt a problem-solving lens. By focusing on significant, real-world problems, investors can identify startups with the potential to create meaningful impact. This approach shifts the emphasis from technology to purpose, allowing investors to evaluate startups based on their ability to address pressing challenges.

For instance, a startup like Dropbox might face stiff competition from industry giants like Amazon and Google, which can leverage their scale and resources to offer similar cloud storage solutions. However, a problem-solving approach would look beyond the specific tool being offered and consider how that tool fits into a larger solution. A startup that addresses a broader problem—such as enabling seamless collaboration across distributed teams—is more likely to succeed in the long term, regardless of competition.

By focusing on problems rather than tools, next-generation tech incubators can identify startups that are resilient and adaptable. These startups are better equipped to navigate market shifts and technological disruptions, as they are not tied to a single solution or approach. Instead, they leverage a range of tools and technologies to achieve their objectives.

The Intersection of Technology and Social Innovation

While technology is a critical enabler of innovation, it is not the only factor that determines success. Social innovation—the development of new approaches to collaboration, governance, and community building—is equally important. Next-generation tech incubators recognize this and strive to foster innovation not just in technology but also in group dynamics and organizational models.

For example, some of the most impactful startups are those that address large-scale societal challenges, such as climate change, healthcare access, and education inequality. These startups often work closely with governments and other stakeholders to implement solutions that have a broad and lasting impact. By fostering collaboration and aligning diverse interests, they create value that extends far beyond financial returns.

The Future of Next-Generation Tech Incubators

As the pace of change continues to accelerate, the role of next-generation tech incubators will become even more critical. These incubators represent a new model of investment, one that goes beyond funding to provide the comprehensive support and ecosystem relationships needed to navigate an increasingly complex innovation landscape.

Looking ahead, the most successful incubators will be those that embrace adaptability and continuous learning. They will adopt new frameworks for evaluating startups, prioritize problem-solving over technology, and foster innovation in both technology and social systems. By doing so, they will not only help startups succeed but also contribute to solving some of the world's most pressing challenges.

In this new era of investment and innovation, next-generation tech incubators are not just catalysts for growth—they are architects of the future. By redefining what it means to support a startup, they are shaping the next wave of technological and societal progress. And in doing so, they are building a foundation for a better, more innovative world.

Part I: The Foundations of a Next-Generation Tech Incubator

Chapter 1: From Checks to Ecosystems

The evolution of investment in the startup ecosystem over the past several decades has been nothing short of transformative. In the early days, investors played a relatively narrow role, offering financial backing and attending occasional board meetings. While this approach laid the groundwork for some iconic companies, it also revealed the limitations of passive investment. As markets became more competitive and innovation accelerated, it became clear that a more comprehensive, hands-on approach was needed. Thus began the shift from checks to ecosystems—a reimagining of how investors support startups in their journey from nascent ideas to transformative enterprises.

The Early Days of Investment: Passive Participation

In the traditional model of investment, the relationship between investors and startups was largely transactional. Founders pitched their ideas to venture capitalists or angel investors, who in turn evaluated the business's potential, negotiated terms, and provided funding. Once the deal was closed, investors typically stepped back, focusing primarily on attending periodic board meetings and monitoring financial performance.

This hands-off approach was, to some extent, a reflection of the era. In the mid-to-late 20th century, the pace of innovation was relatively slower, and startups operated in less crowded and less complex markets. The challenges faced by these companies were often straightforward: securing capital, building a product, and finding customers. As a result, the limited involvement of investors was sufficient in many cases.

However, this model had its shortcomings. Many startups lacked the operational expertise or industry connections needed to navigate the complexities of scaling a business. Founders often found themselves isolated, grappling with challenges they were ill-equipped to handle. The result was a high rate of failure, even among companies with promising ideas and adequate funding.

The Dot-Com Boom and the Need for a New Model

The dot-com boom of the late 1990s and early 2000s marked a turning point in the world of venture capital. The rapid proliferation of internet-based businesses created unprecedented opportunities but also introduced new complexities. Markets became more competitive, customer expectations shifted, and the pace of technological change accelerated. In this environment, the traditional model of passive investment proved inadequate.

The bursting of the dot-com bubble further highlighted the need for a new approach. Many of the companies that failed during this period had received ample funding but lacked the guidance and support needed to build sustainable businesses. This underscored the limitations of writing checks without offering strategic and operational support.

In response, a new model began to emerge. Investors started to take a more active role in supporting their portfolio companies. Rather than merely providing capital, they began offering mentorship, operational assistance, and access to networks of customers, partners, and talent. This shift marked the beginning of the transition from passive participation to active engagement.

The Rise of Ecosystem Thinking

As the investment landscape evolved, it became increasingly clear that startups do not exist in isolation. They are part of a broader ecosystem that includes other startups, investors, corporations, academic institutions, and government entities. Recognizing this, forward-thinking investors began to adopt an ecosystem-based approach, focusing on creating environments where startups could thrive.

An ecosystem-based approach involves more than just providing direct support to individual startups. It also includes fostering connections between different players in the ecosystem, creating opportunities for collaboration, and addressing systemic challenges that hinder innovation. For example, an investor might organize industry-specific events to bring together startups, corporate partners, and regulators. These events can help startups gain valuable insights, establish strategic partnerships, and navigate regulatory hurdles.

This approach has several key benefits. First, it amplifies the impact of investment by leveraging the collective resources and expertise of the ecosystem. Second, it creates a sense of community and shared purpose, which can be particularly valuable for early-stage startups. Finally, it helps address systemic barriers to innovation, such as skill shortages or regulatory bottlenecks.

Beyond Capital: The New Role of Investors

In the ecosystem-based model, the role of investors extends far beyond providing capital. They are now expected to act as mentors, connectors, and enablers, helping startups navigate the complexities of building a business in today's fast-paced, competitive environment.

Mentorship

One of the most important roles that investors play in the ecosystem is that of a mentor. Startups often face a steep learning curve, particularly in the early stages of their journey. Investors with industry experience can provide valuable guidance on a wide range of topics, from product development to market entry strategies.

Mentorship is not a one-size-fits-all proposition. The best investors tailor their advice to the specific needs and challenges of each startup. For example, a startup developing cutting-edge AI technology may need guidance on securing research grants and navigating intellectual property issues, while a consumer-focused e-commerce company might benefit from advice on branding and customer acquisition.

Connecting Startups with Resources

Another critical role of investors in the ecosystem is that of a connector. Startups often need access to resources that go beyond funding, such as talent, customers, and strategic partners. Investors can leverage their networks to help startups access these resources.

For instance, an investor might introduce a startup to a potential corporate partner that can provide access to new markets or offer valuable industry insights. Similarly, they might connect a startup with a seasoned executive who can join the company as a mentor or advisor. These connections can be transformative, enabling startups to overcome barriers and accelerate their growth.

Enabling Collaboration

Collaboration is a cornerstone of the ecosystem-based approach. By fostering collaboration between startups, investors can create opportunities for shared learning and innovation. For example, startups within the same incubator or portfolio might collaborate on joint projects, share insights, or even pool resources to address common challenges.

Investors also play a role in enabling collaboration between startups and other ecosystem players, such as academic institutions and government agencies. For example, an investor might facilitate a partnership between a biotech startup and a research university, enabling the startup to access cutting-edge scientific expertise and facilities.

The Impact of Ecosystem-Based Investing

The shift from checks to ecosystems has had a profound impact on the startup ecosystem. By providing more than just capital, investors have helped startups navigate the complexities of building a business in an increasingly competitive and fast-paced environment. This approach has also contributed to the emergence of a new generation of startups that are more resilient, innovative, and impactful.

One of the key benefits of ecosystem-based investing is that it creates a virtuous cycle of innovation. Startups that succeed within the ecosystem often go on to contribute back to it, either by mentoring other startups, investing in new ventures, or sharing their expertise. This creates a self-sustaining ecosystem that continues to generate value over time.

Moreover, the ecosystem-based approach has made it possible to tackle complex, systemic challenges that no single startup or investor could address alone. By fostering collaboration and leveraging the collective resources of the ecosystem, investors have helped drive innovation in areas such as clean energy, healthcare, and education.

Challenges and Opportunities

While the ecosystem-based approach has many benefits, it also comes with its own set of challenges. Building and maintaining an ecosystem requires significant time, effort, and resources. Investors need to balance the demands of supporting individual startups with the broader goal of fostering a thriving ecosystem.

Additionally, the ecosystem-based approach requires a shift in mindset. Investors need to move away from a transactional view of investment and embrace a more holistic perspective that prioritizes long-term value creation over short-term returns. This can be a difficult transition, particularly for investors who are accustomed to the traditional model.

Despite these challenges, the opportunities presented by the ecosystem-based approach are immense. By adopting this model, investors can create environments where startups can thrive, drive innovation in critical areas, and generate sustainable, long-term value.

Conclusion

The transition from checks to ecosystems represents a fundamental shift in the world of venture capital and startup investing. By adopting an ecosystem-based approach, investors have redefined their role, moving from passive participants to active enablers of innovation. This shift has not only transformed the startup ecosystem but also paved the way for a new era of entrepreneurship, where startups are better equipped to tackle complex challenges and create meaningful impact. As the investment landscape continues to evolve, the ecosystem-based approach will undoubtedly play a central role in shaping the future of innovation.

Chapter 2: Building Support Systems That Thrive

The success of any startup hinges not only on its access to funding but also on the robustness of the support systems that surround it. In the modern era of entrepreneurship, where markets are competitive, innovation cycles are rapid, and customer expectations are continually evolving, startups require more than just financial backing to thrive. They need access to resources, expertise, and infrastructure that enable them to address challenges and seize opportunities at every stage of their journey. This is where the role of support systems becomes critical. The evolution of these systems—from ad-hoc networks to structured, dynamic frameworks—has become a cornerstone of next-generation tech incubators. These systems are designed to not only sustain startups but also propel them toward scalable success in increasingly competitive markets.

The Evolution of Support Systems

Historically, the support systems available to startups were often informal and unstructured. Founders relied on personal networks, mentors, and the occasional industry connection to navigate challenges. While this approach worked for some, it lacked the scalability and consistency needed to support a broader range of startups effectively.

As the startup ecosystem matured, the need for more structured support systems became apparent. Early incubators and accelerators began offering formalized programs that included mentorship, coworking spaces, and access to investor networks. These initiatives marked a significant step forward, but they were often limited in scope and failed to address the diverse needs of startups operating in different industries and stages of growth.

The rise of next-generation tech incubators has brought a new level of sophistication to support systems. These incubators recognize that one-size-fits-all solutions are inadequate in today's dynamic and complex market environment. Instead, they adopt a tailored approach, providing startups with the specific resources and expertise they need to succeed. This shift has transformed the role of support systems from a peripheral aspect of the startup ecosystem to a central pillar of entrepreneurial success.

Key Components of Thriving Support Systems

The support systems provided by next-generation tech incubators are comprehensive and multifaceted, encompassing a wide range of services and resources. These components work together to create an environment where startups can thrive.

1. Mentorship and Expertise

At the heart of any effective support system is access to mentorship and expertise. Startups often face a steep learning curve, particularly in the early stages of their journey. Experienced mentors can provide valuable guidance, helping founders navigate challenges and make informed decisions.

Mentorship programs within incubators are typically tailored to the needs of individual startups. For example, a fintech startup might be paired with mentors who have experience in regulatory compliance and financial services, while a biotech startup might receive guidance from experts in research and development and intellectual property management. This targeted approach ensures that startups receive relevant and actionable advice.

2. Access to Capital

While mentorship and expertise are crucial, access to capital remains a fundamental requirement for startup success. Support systems within incubators often include connections to a network of investors, ranging from venture capitalists to angel investors and corporate partners. These networks provide startups with the funding they need to develop their products, enter new markets, and scale their operations.

Beyond facilitating access to funding, many incubators also provide support in preparing startups for fundraising. This includes assistance with crafting compelling pitch decks, refining business models, and conducting due diligence. By equipping startups with the tools and knowledge they need to secure investment, incubators help them build a strong foundation for growth.

3. Infrastructure and Resources

Startups often operate with limited resources, making access to infrastructure and tools a critical component of support systems. Incubators provide startups with access to coworking spaces, research facilities, and specialized equipment, enabling them to develop and test their products in a cost-effective manner.

For example, a hardware startup might benefit from access to prototyping labs and manufacturing facilities, while a software company might utilize cloud computing resources and data analytics tools. By reducing the barriers to accessing these resources, incubators enable startups to focus on innovation and execution.

4. Talent Development and Recruitment

Attracting and retaining top talent is a significant challenge for startups, particularly in competitive markets. Support systems within incubators often include talent development programs that help startups build high-performing teams. These programs may involve workshops on leadership and team management, access to a pool of skilled professionals, and partnerships with universities and training institutions.

By addressing the talent gap, incubators empower startups to build teams that are capable of executing their vision and driving long-term success.

5. Market Access and Customer Acquisition

For startups, entering new markets and acquiring customers can be daunting tasks. Support systems within incubators provide startups with the tools and connections they need to navigate these challenges. This includes access to market research, introductions to potential customers and partners, and guidance on marketing and sales strategies.

For instance, an incubator might organize industry-specific events where startups can showcase their products to potential customers and investors. These events not only help startups generate leads but also provide valuable feedback that can inform their product development and go-to-market strategies.

6. Community and Collaboration

One of the most valuable aspects of support systems within incubators is the sense of community they create. Startups within an incubator often collaborate and learn from one another, sharing insights, experiences, and resources. This collaborative environment fosters innovation and resilience, helping startups overcome challenges and achieve their goals.

In addition to fostering internal collaboration, incubators also facilitate partnerships with external stakeholders, such as corporations, academic institutions, and government agencies. These partnerships create opportunities for startups to access new resources, enter new markets, and tackle complex challenges that require collective action.

Adapting to Dynamic Market Conditions

In today's fast-paced and ever-changing market environment, the ability to adapt is critical for both startups and the support systems that serve them. Next-generation tech incubators recognize this and have built support systems that are dynamic and responsive to changing conditions.

Evolving Needs of Startups

As startups grow and evolve, their needs change. For example, a startup in the early stages of development might require guidance on product design and prototyping, while a more established company might need support with scaling operations and entering international markets.

Support systems within incubators are designed to adapt to these changing needs. By offering a flexible and tailored approach, incubators ensure that startups receive the right support at the right time. This dynamic approach maximizes the value of the support system and increases the likelihood of startup success.

Embracing New Technologies and Trends

The rapid pace of technological advancement creates both opportunities and challenges for startups. Next-generation tech incubators stay ahead of the curve by continuously updating their support systems to reflect the latest technologies and trends. This includes providing startups with access to cutting-edge tools and resources, as well as offering training programs on emerging technologies.

For example, an incubator might introduce startups to the latest advancements in artificial intelligence, blockchain, or quantum computing, helping them leverage these technologies to gain a competitive edge. By staying at the forefront of innovation, incubators ensure that their support systems remain relevant and effective.

Measuring the Impact of Support Systems

The effectiveness of support systems can be measured in a variety of ways, including the success of the startups they serve, the strength of the ecosystem they create, and the broader impact they have on society.

Startup Success

One of the most direct measures of the effectiveness of support systems is the success of the startups they support. This includes metrics such as revenue growth, market share, customer acquisition, and funding raised. By tracking these metrics, incubators can assess the impact of their support systems and identify areas for improvement.

Ecosystem Strength

Another important measure of effectiveness is the strength of the ecosystem created by the support systems. This includes factors such as the level of collaboration between startups, the diversity of resources available, and the quality of relationships with external stakeholders. A strong ecosystem creates a virtuous cycle of innovation, where successful startups contribute back to the community, creating opportunities for others.

Societal Impact

Beyond individual startup success, the support systems within incubators also have a broader impact on society. By fostering innovation and enabling startups to tackle complex challenges, these systems contribute to economic growth, job creation, and the development of solutions to pressing global issues. Measuring this impact requires a holistic approach that considers both quantitative and qualitative factors.

Conclusion

Building support systems that thrive is essential for the success of startups in today's competitive and fast-paced market environment. By providing startups with access to mentorship, capital, infrastructure, talent, market insights, and a collaborative community, next-generation tech incubators create environments where innovation can flourish. These support systems are dynamic and adaptable, evolving to meet the changing needs of startups and the broader ecosystem.

As the startup ecosystem continues to evolve, the role of support systems will become even more critical. By investing in the development of robust and comprehensive support frameworks, next-generation tech incubators can empower startups to overcome challenges, seize opportunities, and create lasting impact. In doing so, they not only drive entrepreneurial success but also contribute to the advancement of society as a whole.

Chapter 3: Co-Investing for Success

In the rapidly evolving world of entrepreneurship and venture capital, co-investing has emerged as a powerful strategy for driving success. By pooling resources, expertise, and networks, co-investors can amplify the impact of their investments, mitigate risks, and support startups in navigating increasingly complex markets. This chapter delves into the intricacies of co-investing, exploring its benefits, challenges, and best practices. It also examines how next-generation tech incubators leverage co-investing to foster innovation and create value for startups, investors, and the broader ecosystem.

The Concept of Co-Investing

Co-investing refers to the practice of two or more investors jointly funding a startup or venture. This approach has gained popularity in recent years as the startup ecosystem has become more competitive and interconnected. Unlike traditional solo investing, where a single investor provides the majority of funding, co-investing involves collaboration between multiple investors, each contributing capital, expertise, and resources.

At its core, co-investing is about synergy. By working together, investors can achieve outcomes that would be difficult or impossible to accomplish alone. This collaborative approach not only benefits the startups receiving funding but also strengthens the relationships between investors and fosters a sense of shared purpose within the ecosystem.

The Benefits of Co-Investing

Co-investing offers a wide range of benefits for both investors and startups. These benefits are particularly pronounced in the context of next-generation tech incubators, where collaboration and ecosystem-building are central to success.

1. Risk Mitigation

One of the primary advantages of co-investing is the ability to spread risk across multiple investors. Startups are inherently risky ventures, and even the most promising companies can face unexpected challenges. By sharing the financial burden, co-investors can reduce their individual exposure and create a more balanced investment portfolio.

In addition to financial risk, co-investing also mitigates other types of risk, such as market risk and operational risk. For example, an investor with deep industry expertise can help a startup navigate market challenges, while another investor with operational experience can provide guidance on scaling and execution. Together, these investors create a more robust support system for the startup, increasing its chances of success.

2. Access to Diverse Expertise

Co-investing brings together investors with complementary skills, experiences, and networks. This diversity of expertise is invaluable for startups, which often face multifaceted challenges that require a range of perspectives to address effectively.

For instance, a startup in the renewable energy sector might benefit from the combined expertise of an investor with a background in energy markets and another with experience in technology development. By leveraging their collective knowledge, co-investors can provide startups with comprehensive support and strategic guidance.

3. Enhanced Due Diligence

Collaborative due diligence is another significant benefit of co-investing. By pooling their resources and expertise, co-investors can conduct more thorough evaluations of potential investments. This includes analyzing market trends, assessing the startup's competitive position, and evaluating the founding team's capabilities.

Enhanced due diligence not only reduces the risk of making poor investment decisions but also helps startups identify and address potential weaknesses early on. This proactive approach lays the foundation for long-term success.

4. Increased Funding Capacity

Startups often require significant capital to develop their products, enter new markets, and scale their operations. Co-investing allows investors to pool their financial resources, enabling startups to access larger funding rounds without relying on a single investor.

This increased funding capacity is particularly important for startups operating in capital-intensive industries, such as biotechnology, hardware, or infrastructure. By securing sufficient funding, these startups can accelerate their development timelines and compete more effectively in the market.

5. Stronger Ecosystem Relationships

Co-investing fosters collaboration and trust among investors, strengthening the relationships within the ecosystem. These relationships are invaluable for startups, which benefit from the collective resources and networks of their investors.

Moreover, co-investing creates opportunities for investors to learn from one another, share insights, and explore future collaborations. This sense of community enhances the overall health and vibrancy of the ecosystem, creating a virtuous cycle of innovation and success.

The Role of Co-Investing in Tech Incubators

Next-generation tech incubators have embraced co-investing as a core strategy for supporting startups. By facilitating collaborative investments, incubators create an environment where startups can thrive and investors can achieve their goals.

Facilitating Collaborative Investments

Incubators play a critical role in facilitating co-investing by bringing together investors with shared interests and complementary expertise. This involves organizing networking events, investor forums, and pitch sessions where startups can showcase their potential and investors can explore co-investment opportunities.

In addition to matchmaking, incubators also provide a platform for coordinating investment efforts. This includes managing funding rounds, ensuring alignment between co-investors, and addressing any potential conflicts of interest. By streamlining the co-investment process, incubators make it easier for investors to collaborate and for startups to secure the funding they need.

Leveraging Networks and Resources

One of the key advantages of incubator-led co-investing is the ability to leverage the incubator's extensive networks and resources. Incubators often have relationships with a diverse range of stakeholders, including corporate partners, academic institutions, and government agencies. These connections provide co-investors with access to valuable resources and insights that can enhance their investment decisions.

For startups, the benefits are even more pronounced. By securing funding through an incubator, they gain access to a broader ecosystem of support, including mentorship, infrastructure, and market access. This integrated approach increases the likelihood of success and creates value for all stakeholders involved.

Challenges of Co-Investing

While co-investing offers numerous benefits, it also comes with its own set of challenges. These challenges must be carefully managed to ensure the success of collaborative investments.

1. Alignment of Interests

One of the most significant challenges of co-investing is ensuring alignment of interests among investors. Each investor may have different priorities, risk tolerances, and investment horizons, which can lead to conflicts or disagreements.

To address this challenge, it is essential to establish clear expectations and communication channels from the outset. This includes defining the roles and responsibilities of each investor, setting agreed-upon goals and milestones, and creating mechanisms for resolving conflicts.

2. Coordination and Decision-Making

Co-investing requires a high degree of coordination and collaboration among investors. This can be challenging, particularly when multiple investors are involved. Decision-making processes can become cumbersome, leading to delays or inefficiencies.

To overcome this challenge, it is important to establish streamlined decision-making frameworks that allow for timely and effective collaboration. This might involve appointing a lead investor to coordinate efforts or using technology platforms to facilitate communication and information sharing.

3. Managing Risks and Responsibilities

While co-investing reduces individual risk, it also requires investors to share responsibilities and accountability. This can create challenges if one investor fails to meet their obligations or if disagreements arise over the management of the investment.

To mitigate these risks, it is essential to establish clear agreements and governance structures. This includes defining the terms of the co-investment, outlining the responsibilities of each investor, and creating mechanisms for addressing disputes or changes in circumstances.

Best Practices for Successful Co-Investing

To maximize the benefits of co-investing and address its challenges, investors and incubators can adopt a range of best practices.

1. Building Trust and Relationships

Successful co-investing is built on a foundation of trust and strong relationships. Investors should take the time to understand each other's goals, values, and working styles before entering into a co-investment arrangement. This creates a sense of mutual respect and collaboration that is essential for long-term success.

2. Conducting Comprehensive Due Diligence

Thorough due diligence is critical for successful co-investing. This includes not only evaluating the startup's potential but also assessing the capabilities and alignment of co-investors. By conducting comprehensive due diligence, investors can make informed decisions and mitigate potential risks.

3. Establishing Clear Agreements

Clear agreements are essential for managing the complexities of co-investing. These agreements should outline the roles, responsibilities, and expectations of each investor, as well as the terms of the investment and mechanisms for resolving disputes. By establishing clear agreements upfront, investors can avoid misunderstandings and ensure a smooth collaboration.

4. Leveraging Technology and Tools

Technology can play a valuable role in facilitating co-investing. Platforms and tools that enable communication, information sharing, and decision-making can streamline the co-investment process and improve efficiency. By leveraging technology, investors can enhance collaboration and reduce administrative burdens.

5. Adopting a Long-Term Perspective

Co-investing requires a long-term perspective and a commitment to shared success. Investors should focus on building relationships and creating value over time, rather than seeking short-term gains. This approach not only benefits individual investments but also strengthens the broader ecosystem.

Conclusion

Co-investing represents a powerful strategy for driving success in the startup ecosystem. By pooling resources, expertise, and networks, co-investors can amplify their impact, mitigate risks, and create value for startups and the broader ecosystem. Next-generation tech incubators have embraced co-investing as a core component of their approach, facilitating collaborative investments and fostering innovation.

While co-investing comes with its challenges, these can be effectively managed through clear agreements, comprehensive due diligence, and a commitment to collaboration. By adopting best practices and leveraging the strengths of the ecosystem, co-investors can unlock new opportunities and drive meaningful impact. As the startup ecosystem continues to evolve, co-investing will play an increasingly important role in shaping the future of entrepreneurship and innovation.

Part II: Tackling the Challenge of Exponential Innovation

Chapter 4: The Steepening Curve of Innovation

Innovation has always been a driving force behind human progress, but the pace at which it is occurring today is unprecedented. The curve of innovation—a measure of the rate at which new technologies and ideas emerge and disrupt existing paradigms—has steepened dramatically over the past few decades. This acceleration has brought about profound opportunities and challenges for startups, investors, and society as a whole. Understanding the dynamics of this steepening curve is critical for navigating the complexities of the modern innovation landscape.

This chapter explores the factors contributing to the steepening curve of innovation, the implications for startups and ecosystems, and strategies for thriving in an era of exponential change. From the convergence of technologies to the globalization of innovation, we will examine how these forces are reshaping industries and redefining the possibilities of entrepreneurship.

The Exponential Nature of Innovation

A Historical Perspective

Historically, innovation has followed a relatively steady trajectory, punctuated by occasional bursts of rapid advancement. The Industrial Revolution, for example, marked a period of transformative innovation that reshaped economies and societies. Similarly, the advent of the internet in the late 20th century ushered in a new era of connectivity and information exchange.

In the 21st century, however, the pace of innovation has accelerated dramatically. Technologies that once took decades to develop and diffuse are now emerging and scaling at unprecedented speeds. This shift is driven by several key factors, including advances in computing power, the convergence of multiple technologies, and the democratization of innovation.

Moore's Law and Beyond

Moore's Law—the observation that the number of transistors on a microchip doubles approximately every two years—has been a cornerstone of technological progress for decades. This exponential increase in computing power has enabled advancements in fields ranging from artificial intelligence (AI) to biotechnology. While the physical limits of Moore's Law are approaching, the principles of exponential growth continue to drive innovation through alternative technologies such as quantum computing and neuromorphic engineering.

The Convergence of Technologies

One of the most significant drivers of the steepening curve of innovation is the convergence of technologies. Unlike previous eras, where innovation was often confined to isolated domains, today's breakthroughs frequently occur at the intersection of multiple fields. For example:

- **AI and Biotechnology**: AI is accelerating drug discovery and enabling personalized medicine by analyzing vast

datasets and identifying patterns that would be impossible for humans to discern.
- **Blockchain and IoT**: The integration of blockchain technology with the Internet of Things (IoT) is transforming supply chain management, enabling secure and transparent tracking of goods.
- **Renewable Energy and Smart Grids**: Advances in renewable energy technologies, combined with smart grid systems, are revolutionizing the way energy is generated, distributed, and consumed.

These intersections create new possibilities and challenges, as startups must navigate complex ecosystems and collaborate across disciplines to succeed.

The Implications for Startups

The steepening curve of innovation presents both opportunities and challenges for startups. On the one hand, the rapid emergence of new technologies creates a wealth of opportunities for entrepreneurs to develop groundbreaking solutions. On the other hand, the accelerated pace of change increases the pressure on startups to innovate quickly and adapt to shifting market dynamics.

Opportunities in Emerging Technologies

Startups are uniquely positioned to capitalize on emerging technologies, as they are often more agile and risk-tolerant than established corporations. By leveraging the latest advancements, startups can create disruptive solutions that address unmet needs and redefine industries. For example:

- **Healthcare**: Startups are using AI and robotics to improve surgical precision and patient outcomes.

- **Sustainability**: Entrepreneurs are developing innovative solutions for carbon capture, waste reduction, and sustainable agriculture.
- **Education**: EdTech startups are leveraging VR and AI to create immersive and personalized learning experiences.

These opportunities are not limited to technology-driven industries; the principles of innovation can be applied across sectors to create value and drive growth.

Challenges of Rapid Change

While the opportunities are vast, the challenges of navigating the steepening curve of innovation are equally significant. Startups must contend with:

- **Shorter Product Lifecycles**: As technologies evolve rapidly, the lifespan of products and services is shrinking, requiring startups to continually innovate to remain competitive.
- **Intensified Competition**: The democratization of innovation has lowered barriers to entry, increasing competition in many industries.
- **Resource Constraints**: Startups often operate with limited resources, making it difficult to keep pace with larger competitors and rapidly changing market demands.

To succeed in this environment, startups must adopt strategies that enable them to stay ahead of the curve and build sustainable competitive advantages.

Strategies for Thriving in an Era of Exponential Change

To navigate the steepening curve of innovation, startups and investors must embrace new strategies that prioritize adaptability, collaboration, and a problem-solving mindset.

Embracing a Problem-Solving Mindset

In a world of rapid technological change, focusing on solving significant, real-world problems is often more effective than chasing the latest trends. By addressing pressing challenges, startups can create value that transcends technological fads and builds lasting impact.

For example, startups that focus on improving access to clean water, advancing renewable energy, or enhancing public health are likely to find opportunities for growth and impact, regardless of specific technological trends. This problem-solving mindset also enables startups to leverage a wide range of tools and technologies, making them more resilient to market shifts.

Leveraging Ecosystem Collaboration

The complexity of today's innovation landscape requires startups to collaborate with a diverse range of stakeholders, including investors, corporations, academic institutions, and government agencies. By building strong partnerships, startups can access the resources, expertise, and networks needed to succeed.

For instance, a startup developing a new medical device might collaborate with universities for research, partner with hospitals for clinical trials, and work with government agencies to navigate regulatory approvals. These collaborations not only enhance the startup's capabilities but also increase its chances of success.

Prioritizing Agility and Adaptability

In a fast-changing environment, the ability to adapt quickly is a critical determinant of success. Startups must cultivate a culture of agility, where teams are empowered to experiment, learn, and pivot as needed. This requires:

- **Flexible Business Models**: Developing business models that can adapt to changing market conditions and customer needs.
- **Continuous Learning**: Encouraging a mindset of curiosity and lifelong learning to stay informed about emerging trends and technologies.
- **Iterative Development**: Adopting lean methodologies and rapid prototyping to test ideas and refine solutions in real-time.

Investing in Long-Term Resilience

While agility is essential, startups must also focus on building long-term resilience. This involves balancing short-term objectives with strategic investments in areas such as talent development, infrastructure, and organizational culture. By fostering resilience, startups can weather periods of uncertainty and emerge stronger over time.

The Role of Investors in Navigating the Innovation Curve

Investors play a critical role in supporting startups as they navigate the steepening curve of innovation. Beyond providing capital, investors can offer guidance, mentorship, and access to networks that enable startups to thrive.

Identifying High-Potential Opportunities

In an era of exponential change, identifying high-potential opportunities requires a deep understanding of emerging trends and a willingness to take calculated risks. Investors must look beyond the technology itself and evaluate the problem being addressed, the scalability of the solution, and the capabilities of the founding team.

Fostering Collaborative Ecosystems

Investors can enhance the impact of their investments by fostering collaborative ecosystems that bring together diverse stakeholders. By facilitating connections and partnerships, investors create environments where startups can access the resources and support they need to succeed.

Encouraging Long-Term Thinking

While the pace of innovation may incentivize short-term decision-making, investors must encourage startups to adopt a long-term perspective. This involves supporting strategies that prioritize sustainability, ethical considerations, and societal impact alongside financial returns.

Conclusion

The steepening curve of innovation is reshaping the startup ecosystem, creating unprecedented opportunities and challenges for entrepreneurs and investors alike. By understanding the dynamics of this acceleration and adopting strategies that prioritize problem-solving, collaboration, and adaptability, startups can thrive in an era of exponential change. Investors, too, have a critical role to play in supporting this journey, fostering ecosystems that enable innovation and impact.

As the pace of innovation continues to accelerate, the ability to navigate the steepening curve will be a defining factor in the success of startups and the ecosystems that support them. By embracing this challenge, we can unlock the full potential of innovation to drive progress and create a better future.

Chapter 5: The Complexity of Predicting the Future

Predicting the future has always been a challenging endeavor, but in today's world of rapid technological change and interconnected systems, the task has become even more complex. The accelerating pace of innovation, coupled with the convergence of multiple disciplines, has created a landscape where the traditional methods of forecasting are often inadequate. Startups, investors, and ecosystem builders must navigate this uncertainty, balancing the need to anticipate trends with the recognition that the future is inherently unpredictable.

This chapter delves into the intricacies of forecasting in the modern era, exploring the limitations of traditional prediction models, the role of emerging technologies, and the strategies that can help stakeholders better navigate an uncertain future. By understanding the complexity of prediction, we can equip ourselves to make informed decisions and seize opportunities in an ever-changing world.

The Challenge of Complexity

Interconnected Systems and Feedback Loops

One of the key drivers of complexity in modern prediction is the interconnectedness of systems. Technological advancements, economic forces, social dynamics, and environmental factors are increasingly intertwined, creating feedback loops that amplify uncertainty. For example, the adoption of AI in one sector can have cascading effects on labor markets, regulatory policies, and consumer behavior in unrelated industries.

These feedback loops make it difficult to isolate individual variables and predict their outcomes. Traditional models that rely on linear cause-and-effect relationships often fall short in capturing the nuances of these interconnected systems.

The Accelerating Pace of Innovation

The steepening curve of innovation adds another layer of complexity to prediction. Technologies that once took decades to develop and diffuse are now emerging and scaling at unprecedented speeds. This acceleration makes it challenging to anticipate the long-term impact of new technologies, as their adoption and evolution often outpace the ability to analyze them thoroughly.

For example, consider the rapid rise of generative AI. Within a few years, it has transformed industries ranging from content creation to healthcare. Predicting the future trajectory of this technology requires not only an understanding of its current capabilities but also an awareness of how it might intersect with other fields, such as robotics, education, and ethics.

The Role of Uncertainty

Uncertainty is an inherent feature of predicting the future. While data-driven models and historical trends provide valuable insights, they cannot account for unforeseen events or paradigm shifts. Black swan events—highly improbable occurrences with significant impact—are a stark reminder of the limitations of prediction.

The COVID-19 pandemic, for instance, disrupted global economies and accelerated the adoption of remote work, telemedicine, and e-commerce. Few prediction models foresaw the scale and speed of these changes, highlighting the need for adaptability in the face of uncertainty.

Limitations of Traditional Prediction Models

Linear Forecasting

Traditional forecasting models often rely on linear projections, extrapolating past trends into the future. While this approach can be effective in stable environments, it struggles to account for the nonlinear dynamics of today's world. Exponential growth, tipping points, and disruptive innovations frequently render linear models obsolete.

For example, linear models might predict gradual growth in electric vehicle (EV) adoption based on historical sales data. However, they may fail to anticipate breakthroughs in battery technology or regulatory shifts that could accelerate the transition to EVs.

Overreliance on Historical Data

Historical data is a valuable tool for understanding past trends, but it has limitations when applied to future prediction. In a rapidly changing environment, the relevance of historical patterns diminishes. Emerging technologies, shifting consumer preferences, and evolving societal norms can create entirely new trajectories that deviate from historical precedents.

Cognitive Biases

Human decision-making is often influenced by cognitive biases that can distort predictions. Confirmation bias, overconfidence, and anchoring are just a few examples of biases that can lead to inaccurate forecasts. These biases are particularly problematic in complex and uncertain environments, where the need for objective analysis is paramount.

Emerging Approaches to Prediction

While traditional models have their limitations, new approaches are emerging that leverage advanced technologies and methodologies to improve the accuracy and reliability of predictions.

Data-Driven Analytics and Machine Learning

Advances in data analytics and machine learning have revolutionized the field of prediction. By analyzing vast datasets and identifying patterns that are imperceptible to humans, machine learning algorithms can provide valuable insights into future trends.

For example, predictive analytics is widely used in finance to forecast market trends and assess investment risks. Similarly, machine learning models are being applied in healthcare to predict disease outbreaks and optimize treatment plans.

Scenario Planning

Scenario planning is a strategic tool that involves envisioning multiple plausible futures based on different sets of assumptions. Rather than attempting to predict a single outcome, scenario planning encourages stakeholders to consider a range of possibilities and develop strategies that are resilient across various scenarios.

This approach is particularly valuable in uncertain environments, as it allows organizations to prepare for a variety of potential outcomes. For example, a renewable energy startup might develop scenarios based on different rates of regulatory change, technological advancement, and consumer adoption.

Systems Thinking

Systems thinking is an interdisciplinary approach that focuses on understanding the relationships and interactions within complex systems. By considering the broader context and examining how different components influence one another, systems thinking provides a more holistic perspective on prediction.

For example, in the context of urban planning, systems thinking can help stakeholders anticipate the impact of autonomous vehicles on traffic patterns, public transportation, and real estate development.

Crowdsourcing and Collective Intelligence

The collective intelligence of diverse groups can often produce more accurate predictions than individual experts. Crowdsourcing platforms and prediction markets harness the wisdom of the crowd by aggregating insights from a wide range of participants.

For instance, platforms like Metaculus and Good Judgment Project use crowdsourced forecasting to predict outcomes in fields ranging from geopolitics to technology. These platforms demonstrate that diverse perspectives can enhance the accuracy and robustness of predictions.

Strategies for Navigating Uncertainty

Given the inherent complexity of predicting the future, stakeholders must adopt strategies that enable them to navigate uncertainty effectively.

Building Resilience

Resilience is the ability to adapt and thrive in the face of change and uncertainty. For startups, this involves developing flexible business models, cultivating a culture of continuous learning, and building robust networks of support.

For example, a startup operating in the clean energy sector might diversify its revenue streams by offering both hardware solutions (e.g., solar panels) and software services (e.g., energy management platforms). This diversification reduces the company's reliance on a single market or technology, enhancing its resilience to unexpected disruptions.

Embracing Experimentation

Experimentation is a critical tool for navigating uncertainty. By testing hypotheses, iterating on ideas, and learning from failures, organizations can reduce the risks associated with uncertainty and discover new opportunities.

Lean methodologies, such as rapid prototyping and A/B testing, are particularly valuable for startups seeking to innovate in dynamic environments. These approaches enable startups to validate their assumptions and refine their offerings based on real-world feedback.

Fostering Collaboration

Collaboration is essential for addressing the complexity of modern prediction. By working together, stakeholders can pool their expertise, share resources, and co-create solutions that are greater than the sum of their parts.

For example, a biotech startup might collaborate with academic researchers, regulatory agencies, and pharmaceutical companies to accelerate the development and commercialization of a new treatment. These partnerships enhance the startup's capabilities and increase the likelihood of success.

Leveraging Adaptive Leadership

Adaptive leadership is a framework that emphasizes flexibility, resilience, and the ability to navigate change. Leaders who embrace this approach are open to new ideas, willing to take calculated risks, and adept at managing ambiguity.

For instance, an adaptive leader in a tech startup might prioritize cross-functional collaboration, encourage experimentation, and foster a culture of continuous improvement. These practices enable the organization to respond effectively to shifting market dynamics and emerging opportunities.

The Role of Ecosystems in Prediction

Ecosystems play a critical role in shaping the ability of startups and investors to navigate uncertainty. By fostering collaboration, providing access to resources, and facilitating knowledge exchange, ecosystems create an environment where prediction and innovation can thrive.

Knowledge Sharing and Learning

Ecosystems provide a platform for sharing knowledge and learning from diverse perspectives. Industry conferences, incubator programs, and collaborative networks enable stakeholders to exchange insights, identify trends, and build a collective understanding of emerging opportunities.

Access to Resources

Ecosystems also provide startups with access to resources that enhance their predictive capabilities. This includes access to data, analytical tools, and expertise in areas such as market research, technology development, and regulatory compliance.

Building Trust and Collaboration

Trust is a foundational element of effective ecosystems. By fostering trust among stakeholders, ecosystems enable the open exchange of information and the development of collaborative strategies. This sense of community enhances the ability of stakeholders to navigate uncertainty and drive collective success.

Conclusion

Predicting the future is an inherently complex and uncertain endeavor, but it is also an essential part of navigating the modern innovation landscape. By understanding the limitations of traditional prediction models and embracing new approaches, stakeholders can enhance their ability to anticipate trends and seize opportunities.

From leveraging data-driven analytics and scenario planning to fostering collaboration and resilience, the strategies outlined in this chapter provide a roadmap for navigating uncertainty. As the pace of change continues to accelerate, the ability to adapt and thrive in an unpredictable world will be a defining factor in the success of startups, investors, and ecosystems alike.

Chapter 6: The Problem-Solving Lens

In an era defined by rapid technological advancements and complex global challenges, the ability to solve real-world problems has emerged as a critical determinant of success for startups, investors, and ecosystems. Shifting the focus from building tools to solving problems represents a fundamental change in how innovation is approached and executed. A problem-solving lens emphasizes purpose over technology, addressing significant needs in ways that create lasting impact and value.

This chapter explores the importance of adopting a problem-solving mindset in the startup ecosystem. It delves into the principles of problem-centric innovation, the advantages of this approach, and the strategies for effectively identifying and addressing problems. Additionally, it examines the role of ecosystems and investors in fostering a problem-solving culture and the broader implications for society.

The Shift from Tools to Problems

Understanding the Tool-Centric Approach

Traditionally, much of innovation has been driven by the creation of tools—technologies, products, or services designed to address specific functions or tasks. While tools can be powerful enablers, they are often limited in scope and may fail to address the underlying problems they aim to solve. For example:

- **Cloud Storage**: Early solutions like Dropbox revolutionized file sharing and storage, but they faced challenges as larger players like Google and Amazon entered the market with integrated ecosystems and broader capabilities.
- **Fitness Trackers**: Devices like pedometers and basic fitness bands provided data but did not necessarily improve health outcomes without addressing behavioral or systemic factors.

These examples illustrate the limitations of focusing solely on tools without considering the broader context or the deeper problems they aim to address.

Embracing a Problem-Solving Mindset

A problem-solving mindset shifts the focus from the tool itself to the need it addresses. This approach prioritizes understanding the problem, exploring its root causes, and developing comprehensive solutions that create meaningful impact. For instance:

- A startup focused on education might go beyond building e-learning platforms to address barriers like internet accessibility, teacher training, or curriculum design.
- In healthcare, a problem-solving approach might involve tackling underlying issues such as affordability, preventive care, or health literacy rather than simply offering new diagnostic tools.

By centering on problems, innovators can create solutions that are more impactful, resilient, and adaptable to changing circumstances.

The Principles of Problem-Centric Innovation

1. Deep Empathy and Understanding

At the heart of problem-solving is a deep understanding of the people and contexts involved. This requires empathy, active listening, and immersion in the problem space. Successful innovators invest time in understanding the needs, aspirations, and pain points of their target audience.

For example, a startup aiming to improve financial inclusion might conduct extensive field research in underserved communities, exploring the challenges faced by individuals without access to traditional banking systems.

2. Systems Thinking

Problems rarely exist in isolation; they are part of larger, interconnected systems. Systems thinking involves analyzing the relationships and dynamics within these systems to identify leverage points and potential solutions.

For instance, addressing urban traffic congestion requires considering factors such as public transportation, urban planning, environmental impact, and commuter behavior.

3. Iterative Experimentation

Problem-solving is inherently iterative. Innovators must test hypotheses, gather feedback, and refine their approaches based on real-world results. This process requires a willingness to learn from failures and adapt to new insights.

Lean startup methodologies, which emphasize rapid prototyping and continuous improvement, are well-suited to this iterative approach.

4. Collaboration and Co-Creation

Many of today's most pressing problems are too complex to be solved by any single organization or individual. Collaboration and co-creation bring together diverse perspectives, resources, and expertise to develop holistic solutions.

For example, a startup working on climate change mitigation might collaborate with policymakers, scientists, and industry leaders to develop scalable and impactful initiatives.

The Advantages of a Problem-Solving Lens

1. Resilience and Adaptability

Solutions that address fundamental problems are more resilient to changes in technology, market dynamics, or competition. By focusing on the underlying need, startups can pivot more effectively and maintain relevance over time.

For instance, a startup focused on improving access to education can adapt its delivery methods—from in-person workshops to digital platforms—as technology and circumstances evolve.

2. Competitive Differentiation

A problem-solving approach helps startups stand out in crowded markets by offering solutions that are truly aligned with customer needs. This differentiation builds trust, loyalty, and long-term value.

For example, Tesla's focus on sustainable transportation has differentiated it from traditional automakers, positioning the company as a leader in addressing climate change.

3. Broader Impact

Problem-solving extends beyond immediate business goals to create broader social, economic, and environmental impact.

Startups that address significant challenges contribute to societal progress while building sustainable businesses.

Strategies for Identifying and Addressing Problems

1. Conducting Root Cause Analysis

Effective problem-solving begins with identifying the root causes of a challenge rather than addressing its symptoms. Tools like the "5 Whys" technique or fishbone diagrams can help teams explore the underlying factors behind a problem.

For instance, a startup aiming to reduce hospital readmissions might identify root causes such as inadequate patient education, poor follow-up care, or socioeconomic barriers to treatment adherence.

2. Engaging Stakeholders

Involving stakeholders—customers, partners, and communities—in the problem-solving process ensures that solutions are relevant, inclusive, and effective. Stakeholder engagement provides valuable insights and fosters buy-in for the proposed solution.

3. Leveraging Data and Insights

Data-driven decision-making is a critical component of problem-solving. By analyzing quantitative and qualitative data, startups can identify patterns, measure impact, and refine their strategies.

For example, a company addressing food waste might use data analytics to identify inefficiencies in supply chains, optimize inventory management, and reduce waste at scale.

4. Prototyping and Testing

Prototyping and testing enable startups to validate their assumptions and iterate on their solutions. By experimenting in controlled environments and gathering user feedback, innovators can refine their approaches and increase the likelihood of success.

5. Scaling Solutions

Once a solution is validated, scaling becomes the next challenge. This involves adapting the solution to new contexts, expanding reach, and ensuring sustainability. Partnerships and ecosystem support are often critical for successful scaling.

The Role of Ecosystems and Investors

Fostering a Problem-Solving Culture

Ecosystems play a vital role in promoting a problem-solving mindset. By fostering collaboration, providing resources, and celebrating impact-driven innovation, ecosystems create an environment where problem-solving thrives.

Aligning Investment with Purpose

Investors have a unique opportunity to drive problem-solving by aligning their capital with purpose-driven ventures. Impact investing, which prioritizes social and environmental outcomes alongside financial returns, exemplifies this approach.

Encouraging Long-Term Thinking

A problem-solving lens encourages long-term thinking, which aligns with sustainable growth and societal progress. By prioritizing enduring impact over short-term gains, ecosystems and investors can support startups in creating meaningful change.

The Broader Implications of Problem-Solving

Adopting a problem-solving lens has profound implications for society. It shifts the focus of innovation from incremental improvements to transformative solutions that address the world's most pressing challenges. By aligning entrepreneurial efforts with societal needs, the problem-solving approach creates a future where technology and business serve as forces for good.

Conclusion

The problem-solving lens represents a powerful paradigm shift in the startup ecosystem. By prioritizing purpose over technology and addressing significant challenges with empathy, systems thinking, and collaboration, startups can create solutions that deliver lasting value. Ecosystems and investors have a critical role to play in fostering this mindset, supporting innovators in their quest to tackle complex problems and drive meaningful impact.

In an increasingly interconnected and rapidly changing world, the ability to solve real-world problems is not just a competitive advantage—it is a necessity. By embracing this approach, we can unlock the full potential of innovation to create a better, more equitable, and sustainable future.

Part III: Tools, Trends, and Transformation

Chapter 7: The Role of Tools in Problem-Solving

Innovation has long been driven by the development of tools—products, technologies, and services designed to enhance efficiency, solve problems, or unlock new opportunities. Yet, the true power of tools lies not merely in their creation but in their effective application to address real-world challenges. In today's dynamic landscape of exponential innovation, the role of tools has expanded, requiring entrepreneurs, investors, and ecosystems to reevaluate how tools are developed, adopted, and integrated into solutions.

This chapter explores the evolving role of tools in problem-solving, examining their significance in innovation, the risks of tool-centric thinking, and the strategies for aligning tools with purpose-driven solutions. It also highlights examples of how tools have shaped industries and society while underscoring the importance of context, adaptability, and collaboration in maximizing their impact.

The Evolution of Tools in Innovation

From Utility to Empowerment

Historically, tools have been designed to fulfill specific functions, addressing narrow and immediate needs. Early inventions like the wheel, plow, and printing press revolutionized human productivity, setting the stage for subsequent waves of innovation. Over time, tools have evolved from simple instruments to complex systems, enabling individuals and organizations to tackle increasingly sophisticated challenges.

In the digital age, tools are no longer limited to physical artifacts. Software platforms, algorithms, and networks have emerged as transformative enablers of innovation. For example:

- **Cloud Computing**: Platforms like AWS and Azure provide scalable infrastructure, empowering startups to build and deploy applications without the need for extensive hardware investments.
- **Artificial Intelligence**: Machine learning algorithms enhance decision-making, automate processes, and unlock insights from vast datasets.
- **Collaboration Tools**: Platforms like Slack and Zoom facilitate remote work and global collaboration, transforming how teams communicate and operate.

These advancements demonstrate how tools have shifted from merely enhancing utility to empowering creativity, connectivity, and problem-solving.

The Rise of Ecosystem-Driven Tools

The role of tools has also expanded through their integration into ecosystems. Unlike standalone solutions, ecosystem-driven tools operate within interconnected networks, enabling synergies across industries and disciplines. For instance:

- **IoT Devices**: Internet of Things (IoT) devices collect and share data, creating opportunities for cross-industry applications in areas like smart cities, healthcare, and agriculture.
- **Blockchain Technology**: Blockchain enables decentralized, secure transactions and record-keeping, with

applications ranging from supply chain management to digital identity.
- **APIs and Open Platforms**: Application Programming Interfaces (APIs) allow tools to interoperate, fostering innovation through modularity and interoperability.

This ecosystem-centric approach amplifies the impact of tools by leveraging collective capabilities and fostering collaboration.

The Risks of Tool-Centric Thinking

While tools are essential to innovation, an overemphasis on their creation can lead to several pitfalls. Tool-centric thinking, which prioritizes the development of tools over their application to meaningful problems, risks undermining the broader goals of innovation.

The "Build It and They Will Come" Fallacy

One common pitfall of tool-centric thinking is the assumption that creating a new tool will automatically generate demand. While innovative tools can capture attention, their success often depends on their alignment with real-world needs. For example:

- A startup developing a cutting-edge wearable device might struggle if it fails to address consumer pain points such as affordability, usability, or integration with existing ecosystems.
- Similarly, a software platform offering advanced features may face low adoption if it overlooks user experience or lacks a compelling value proposition.

Fragmentation and Redundancy

Another risk of tool-centric thinking is the proliferation of fragmented or redundant solutions. In competitive markets, multiple players often develop similar tools, leading to overcrowding and inefficiencies. For example, the surge of fintech apps offering overlapping functionalities has created confusion among consumers and diluted the impact of individual innovations.

Misalignment with Societal Needs

Focusing exclusively on tools can also result in missed opportunities to address pressing societal challenges. For instance, tools designed to optimize e-commerce logistics may prioritize convenience over sustainability, exacerbating environmental issues. A problem-solving approach, by contrast, considers the broader context and seeks to align tools with ethical and societal goals.

Aligning Tools with Problem-Solving

To maximize the impact of tools, innovators must adopt a problem-solving lens, ensuring that tools are designed, deployed, and scaled in ways that address meaningful challenges.

1. Understanding the Problem Context

Effective problem-solving begins with a deep understanding of the problem context. This involves analyzing the needs, constraints, and dynamics of the target environment. Tools should be tailored to the specific conditions in which they will operate, taking into account cultural, economic, and technological factors.

For example, solar-powered lighting solutions developed for off-grid communities must consider affordability, durability, and maintenance requirements to ensure successful adoption.

2. Prioritizing User-Centric Design

User-centric design ensures that tools are intuitive, accessible, and aligned with user needs. By involving end-users in the design process, innovators can create solutions that resonate with their target audience and drive adoption.

For instance, mobile payment platforms like M-Pesa achieved widespread success in developing regions by prioritizing simplicity and addressing the needs of unbanked populations.

3. Leveraging Data and Insights

Data-driven insights play a crucial role in aligning tools with problems. By analyzing user behavior, market trends, and system performance, innovators can refine their tools and optimize their impact.

For example, predictive analytics in agriculture enables farmers to make data-informed decisions, improving crop yields and resource efficiency.

4. Building Flexibility and Scalability

Tools should be designed with flexibility and scalability in mind, allowing them to adapt to evolving needs and expand their reach. Modular architectures, open standards, and iterative development processes enable tools to grow and evolve over time.

For instance, modular electric vehicle platforms allow automakers to customize vehicles for different markets and use cases, enhancing scalability and cost efficiency.

The Role of Collaboration and Ecosystems

Collaboration and ecosystem engagement are critical for maximizing the impact of tools. By integrating tools into broader systems and fostering partnerships, innovators can amplify their reach and effectiveness.

Ecosystem Integration

Tools that operate within ecosystems benefit from synergies and network effects. For example, health-tech startups that integrate their solutions with electronic health record (EHR) systems can streamline workflows for providers and improve patient outcomes.

Cross-Sector Collaboration

Collaborating across sectors enhances the versatility and impact of tools. For instance, partnerships between tech companies, nonprofits, and governments have enabled the development of tools for disaster response, such as early warning systems and resource coordination platforms.

Open Innovation

Open innovation models encourage collaboration and knowledge sharing, enabling tools to benefit from collective expertise. Open-source software projects like Linux and Kubernetes exemplify how collaborative development can drive widespread adoption and continuous improvement.

Case Studies: Tools That Transformed Industries

1. The Smartphone Revolution

The smartphone exemplifies how a versatile tool can transform multiple industries. By combining communication, computing, and connectivity, smartphones have become essential platforms for applications ranging from navigation to health monitoring. Their impact extends beyond convenience, driving innovation in fields such as telemedicine, e-learning, and e-commerce.

2. AI in Healthcare

AI-powered tools are revolutionizing healthcare by enhancing diagnostics, optimizing treatment plans, and enabling personalized medicine. For example, AI algorithms analyze medical images to detect conditions like cancer with unprecedented accuracy, improving outcomes and reducing costs.

3. Renewable Energy Technologies

Tools like photovoltaic panels, wind turbines, and energy storage systems are driving the transition to sustainable energy. By addressing challenges such as cost, efficiency, and grid integration, these tools are reshaping the global energy landscape.

The Future of Tools in Problem-Solving

As the pace of innovation accelerates, the role of tools in problem-solving will continue to evolve. Emerging trends and technologies, such as quantum computing, synthetic biology, and decentralized networks, hold immense potential to address complex challenges. However, realizing this potential requires a commitment to aligning tools with purpose and context.

Conclusion

Tools are powerful enablers of innovation, but their true value lies in their ability to address real-world problems. By shifting the focus from tool-centric thinking to problem-solving, innovators can create solutions that are impactful, resilient, and aligned with societal needs. Collaboration, ecosystem engagement, and a user-centric approach are essential for maximizing the impact of tools and driving meaningful change.

In the quest to solve humanity's most pressing challenges, tools will remain indispensable—but only when wielded with purpose and insight. By embracing this perspective, startups, investors, and ecosystems can harness the transformative potential of tools to create a better, more sustainable future.

Chapter 8: Governments as Clients and Partners

Governments play a pivotal role in shaping the trajectory of innovation. As regulators, funders, and service providers, they influence markets, drive policy, and address societal challenges at scale. For startups, engaging with governments as clients and partners represents a unique opportunity to tackle large-scale problems, gain credibility, and achieve sustainable growth. However, working with governments also comes with its own set of challenges, requiring a nuanced understanding of public-sector dynamics and strategic collaboration.

This chapter explores the role of governments as clients and partners, examining the opportunities and challenges of working with public-sector entities. It delves into strategies for startups to engage effectively with governments, the benefits of public-private partnerships, and the broader implications of government collaboration for innovation ecosystems and societal progress.

The Importance of Governments in Innovation

Governments as Drivers of Demand

Governments are among the largest buyers of goods and services in the world. From infrastructure projects to healthcare systems, public-sector spending represents a significant portion of global economic activity. For startups, government contracts provide access to stable, large-scale revenue streams that can fuel growth and innovation.

For example:

- **Defense and Security**: Governments invest heavily in defense technologies, cybersecurity, and intelligence systems, creating opportunities for startups specializing in these areas.
- **Public Health**: Initiatives such as vaccine distribution, telemedicine, and health data management rely on innovative solutions developed in collaboration with private-sector partners.
- **Infrastructure and Sustainability**: Smart city projects, renewable energy initiatives, and transportation systems often involve partnerships between governments and technology providers.

Governments as Regulators and Policymakers

In addition to being major buyers, governments shape markets through regulation and policy. Their decisions can accelerate the adoption of new technologies, create incentives for innovation, and address market failures. For instance:

- Subsidies and tax credits for renewable energy have driven the adoption of solar and wind power.
- Data privacy regulations like GDPR have influenced the development of cybersecurity and data management solutions.
- Investments in broadband infrastructure have expanded access to digital services in underserved regions.

Startups that align with government priorities and comply with regulatory requirements are better positioned to succeed in these markets.

Governments as Ecosystem Enablers

Governments also play a critical role in fostering innovation ecosystems. Through funding programs, research grants, and incubators, they support the development of new technologies and encourage entrepreneurship. Public-sector investments in areas like space exploration, quantum computing, and AI research have catalyzed breakthroughs that benefit both public and private sectors.

Opportunities for Startups in Public-Sector Engagement

1. Access to Large-Scale Contracts

Government contracts provide startups with access to significant funding and long-term revenue streams. Winning a public-sector contract can validate a startup's value proposition, enhance its credibility, and open doors to new opportunities.

For example, startups specializing in drone technology have secured lucrative contracts with defense agencies for surveillance and logistics applications.

2. Solving High-Impact Problems

Governments tackle some of society's most pressing challenges, such as climate change, public health, and infrastructure development. By collaborating with governments, startups can contribute to solutions that have far-reaching societal impact.

For instance, a startup focused on water purification technology might partner with governments to address water scarcity in developing regions.

3. Leveraging Public Funding and Resources

Many governments offer funding programs, grants, and incentives to support startups. These resources can help startups overcome financial barriers, accelerate product development, and scale their operations.

For example, programs like the U.S. Small Business Innovation Research (SBIR) grant provide early-stage funding for startups developing cutting-edge technologies.

4. Building Credibility and Market Access

A partnership or contract with a government entity can enhance a startup's reputation and credibility. This validation can facilitate entry into new markets, attract investors, and build trust with other stakeholders.

For example, a startup providing cybersecurity solutions that partners with a government agency may gain recognition as a reliable and secure provider, attracting additional clients in the private sector.

Challenges of Working with Governments

While the opportunities are significant, working with governments also presents unique challenges. Startups must navigate bureaucratic processes, comply with stringent requirements, and adapt to the slower pace of public-sector decision-making.

1. Lengthy Procurement Processes

Government procurement processes are often complex and time-consuming, involving multiple stages of evaluation, negotiation, and approval. Startups must be prepared to invest time and resources in navigating these processes.

2. Compliance and Regulatory Burdens

Governments impose strict compliance requirements to ensure accountability, security, and fairness. Startups must meet these standards, which can be resource-intensive and challenging for early-stage companies.

For instance, startups working with defense agencies may need to comply with cybersecurity standards and obtain security clearances.

3. Risk of Political and Economic Instability

Government budgets and priorities can shift due to political changes, economic conditions, or unforeseen crises. Startups relying heavily on government contracts must be prepared for potential disruptions.

4. Balancing Innovation with Public Accountability

Governments prioritize transparency, accountability, and equity, which can sometimes limit the flexibility and speed of innovation. Startups must navigate these constraints while delivering solutions that meet public-sector expectations.

Strategies for Engaging with Governments

1. Understanding Government Priorities

To engage effectively with governments, startups must understand their priorities, challenges, and goals. This involves researching policy agendas, budget allocations, and procurement trends to identify areas of alignment.

For example, a startup developing AI solutions for healthcare might focus on government initiatives to improve public health outcomes and reduce costs.

2. Building Relationships and Networks

Establishing relationships with government officials, agencies, and industry stakeholders is critical for navigating the public-sector landscape. Networking events, industry conferences, and public-private forums provide opportunities to connect with decision-makers.

3. Demonstrating Value and Impact

Governments prioritize solutions that deliver measurable value and impact. Startups must clearly articulate how their offerings address public-sector challenges, align with policy goals, and generate positive outcomes for citizens.

4. Leveraging Partnerships

Collaborating with established companies, research institutions, or nonprofit organizations can enhance a startup's credibility and capacity to deliver solutions. Partnerships can also help startups navigate complex procurement processes and scale their impact.

5. Preparing for Compliance and Scalability

Startups must invest in building the infrastructure, processes, and capabilities required to meet government standards. This includes developing robust security protocols, ensuring regulatory compliance, and demonstrating scalability.

The Role of Public-Private Partnerships

Public-private partnerships (PPPs) are a powerful mechanism for addressing societal challenges by combining the strengths of governments and private-sector entities. PPPs enable startups to collaborate with governments on large-scale projects, leveraging shared resources and expertise.

Examples of Successful PPPs

- **Smart Cities**: Collaborations between governments and technology providers have enabled the development of

smart city initiatives, such as IoT-enabled infrastructure and energy-efficient systems.
- **Healthcare Innovation**: Public-private partnerships have accelerated the development and distribution of vaccines, medical devices, and telemedicine solutions.
- **Sustainability Projects**: Startups working on renewable energy and environmental conservation have partnered with governments to implement large-scale sustainability initiatives.

Benefits of PPPs

- **Resource Sharing**: PPPs leverage the combined resources of public and private entities, enabling the execution of ambitious projects.
- **Risk Mitigation**: By sharing risks, PPPs reduce the financial and operational burden on individual stakeholders.
- **Scalability**: Partnerships enable startups to scale their solutions to reach larger populations and address systemic challenges.

Broader Implications of Government Collaboration

Engaging with governments as clients and partners has far-reaching implications for innovation ecosystems and societal progress. By aligning entrepreneurial efforts with public-sector goals, startups can drive meaningful change and contribute to sustainable development.

Advancing Societal Goals

Government collaboration enables startups to address critical challenges such as healthcare access, climate change, and education inequality. By focusing on solutions with societal impact, startups contribute to progress that benefits communities and economies.

Strengthening Innovation Ecosystems

Startups that engage with governments often catalyze broader ecosystem development. Their success inspires other entrepreneurs, attracts investment, and fosters collaboration between public and private stakeholders.

Enhancing Public Trust in Innovation

By delivering solutions that improve public services and address societal needs, startups can build trust in the value of innovation. This trust fosters greater acceptance of new technologies and encourages continued investment in research and development.

Conclusion

Governments are indispensable partners in the journey of innovation. For startups, engaging with public-sector entities offers opportunities to solve high-impact problems, access large-scale funding, and build credibility. While the challenges of navigating bureaucracy, compliance, and political dynamics are significant, the rewards of government collaboration—both for startups and society—are immense.

By adopting strategies that prioritize alignment with government priorities, demonstrate value, and foster partnerships, startups can unlock the full potential of public-sector engagement. In doing so, they contribute not only to their own growth but also to the advancement of society as a whole. Governments, in turn, benefit from the agility, creativity, and technological expertise of startups, creating a symbiotic relationship that drives progress and innovation at scale.

Chapter 9: Innovation Beyond Technology

Innovation is often associated with technological advancements, from artificial intelligence to renewable energy solutions. While technology remains a critical driver of progress, it is only one piece of the broader puzzle. True innovation extends beyond technological breakthroughs, encompassing areas such as organizational design, group dynamics, policy-making, and societal structures. These "non-technical" aspects of innovation are just as crucial in addressing complex challenges, fostering collaboration, and driving sustainable growth.

This chapter explores the dimensions of innovation that go beyond technology. It examines the importance of organizational and social innovation, the role of leadership and culture in fostering creativity, and the ways in which ecosystems can support innovation in these non-technical domains. Through examples and strategies, we aim to illuminate the transformative potential of innovation when it transcends technological boundaries.

The Broader Definition of Innovation

Redefining the Concept

Traditionally, innovation has been equated with the development of new products, services, or technologies. However, this definition overlooks the significance of innovations in processes, structures, and relationships. Broader definitions of innovation include:

- **Organizational Innovation**: Redesigning structures, workflows, or incentives to improve efficiency, adaptability, or employee satisfaction.
- **Social Innovation**: Developing solutions to societal challenges, such as inequality, education gaps, or public health crises.

- **Policy Innovation**: Crafting policies that address systemic issues and create an enabling environment for progress.

These forms of innovation are interconnected, often complementing technological advancements to create holistic solutions.

The Interplay Between Technology and Non-Technological Innovation

While technology is a powerful enabler, its impact is often limited without accompanying innovations in other domains. For example:

- The widespread adoption of remote work technologies during the COVID-19 pandemic required organizational innovation, such as rethinking team management, communication norms, and work-life balance.
- Advances in renewable energy technologies are amplified by policy innovations, such as carbon pricing and green subsidies, that incentivize adoption.
- Breakthroughs in healthcare, such as telemedicine, depend on social innovations like improving digital literacy and equitable access to devices.

This interplay highlights the need for a multi-faceted approach to innovation.

Organizational Innovation

Rethinking Structures and Processes

Organizational innovation involves reimagining the way companies and institutions operate. This can include flattening hierarchies, fostering cross-functional collaboration, or adopting agile methodologies. Examples include:

- **Holacracy**: Companies like Zappos have experimented with decentralized management systems, empowering employees to take ownership of decisions.
- **Agile Frameworks**: Originally developed for software development, agile methodologies are now applied across industries to enhance adaptability and responsiveness.

Building Inclusive and Collaborative Cultures

An organization's culture plays a pivotal role in its capacity to innovate. Inclusive cultures that value diverse perspectives, encourage experimentation, and tolerate failure are more likely to foster creativity. Strategies for cultivating such cultures include:

- Encouraging open communication and psychological safety.
- Recognizing and rewarding innovative ideas.
- Providing opportunities for continuous learning and development.

The Role of Leadership

Effective leadership is essential for driving organizational innovation. Transformational leaders inspire teams, articulate a compelling vision, and create an environment where innovation thrives. Characteristics of innovative leaders include:

- Willingness to take calculated risks.
- Ability to navigate ambiguity and adapt to change.
- Commitment to building trust and fostering collaboration.

Social Innovation

Addressing Societal Challenges

Social innovation focuses on creating solutions to pressing societal problems, often through grassroots initiatives, partnerships, or community-driven approaches. Examples include:

- **Microfinance**: Organizations like Grameen Bank have pioneered financial inclusion by providing small loans to underserved communities.
- **Education Innovations**: Initiatives such as Khan Academy have democratized access to quality education through free online resources.
- **Healthcare Access**: Social enterprises like OneWorld Health address healthcare disparities in low-income regions.

Leveraging Cross-Sector Collaboration

Social innovation often requires collaboration between governments, nonprofits, and private-sector organizations. By pooling resources and expertise, these partnerships can tackle challenges at scale. For example:

- Public-private partnerships in disaster response have enabled faster and more effective delivery of aid.
- Collaborative models in urban planning have fostered sustainable city development by integrating diverse stakeholder perspectives.

Measuring Impact

Social innovation demands a focus on outcomes rather than outputs. Metrics such as improved quality of life, increased equity, or enhanced community resilience are more relevant than traditional financial indicators. Tools like social return on investment (SROI) and impact assessments can help measure progress.

Policy Innovation

Creating an Enabling Environment

Policy innovation involves designing regulatory frameworks and incentives that drive progress while addressing systemic barriers. Examples include:

- **Carbon Pricing**: Policies that internalize the environmental costs of carbon emissions encourage the adoption of cleaner technologies.
- **Open Data Initiatives**: Governments that release anonymized data sets for public use spur innovation in areas like transportation, healthcare, and education.
- **Regulatory Sandboxes**: These environments allow startups to test innovative solutions in a controlled setting, fostering experimentation while managing risks.

Engaging Stakeholders

Effective policy innovation requires input from a diverse range of stakeholders, including citizens, businesses, and advocacy groups. Participatory approaches, such as public consultations and co-creation workshops, ensure that policies are inclusive and responsive.

Balancing Innovation with Equity

Policies must balance the need for innovation with the imperative to ensure fairness and accessibility. For example, digital transformation initiatives should address the digital divide by investing in infrastructure and skills development for marginalized communities.

Ecosystem Support for Non-Technical Innovation

Building Collaborative Networks

Innovation ecosystems thrive when stakeholders from different domains work together. Incubators, accelerators, and innovation hubs can foster cross-sector collaboration by bringing together entrepreneurs, researchers, policymakers, and community leaders.

Providing Resources and Incentives

Ecosystems must provide the resources needed to support non-technical innovation. This includes:

- Funding for social enterprises and policy research.
- Platforms for knowledge sharing and capacity building.
- Recognition programs that celebrate achievements in non-technical innovation.

Encouraging Experimentation and Iteration

Non-technical innovation often involves navigating ambiguity and testing new approaches. Ecosystems can support this process by creating safe spaces for experimentation, such as pilot programs and living labs.

Case Studies: Innovation Beyond Technology

1. Denmark's Energy Transition

Denmark's leadership in renewable energy is not only a result of technological advancements but also policy and social innovations. Collaborative energy planning, citizen engagement, and supportive regulations have enabled the country to achieve a high share of wind power in its energy mix.

2. The Mondragon Cooperative

The Mondragon Corporation in Spain exemplifies organizational innovation. As a worker-owned cooperative, it fosters inclusive decision-making, equitable profit-sharing, and resilience through diversification.

3. Participatory Budgeting in Brazil

Participatory budgeting initiatives in Brazilian cities allow citizens to have a direct say in how public funds are allocated. This social innovation has increased transparency, accountability, and community empowerment.

The Future of Innovation Beyond Technology

As global challenges become more complex, the importance of non-technical innovation will only grow. The future will require:

- Greater integration of technological and non-technical approaches.
- Expanded focus on systemic solutions that address root causes.
- Ongoing collaboration across sectors and disciplines.

Conclusion

Innovation beyond technology is a vital component of progress. By reimagining organizational structures, addressing societal challenges, and crafting forward-thinking policies, we can create solutions that are both impactful and sustainable. Ecosystems, leaders, and communities must embrace a holistic approach to innovation, recognizing the value of non-technical advancements in driving meaningful change.

Through collaboration, creativity, and a commitment to addressing real-world problems, innovation beyond technology has the potential to reshape industries, improve lives, and build a more equitable and resilient future.

Part IV: The Future of Next-Generation Incubators

Chapter 10: Rethinking Metrics of Success

In the traditional business landscape, success has often been defined by financial metrics such as revenue growth, profitability, and shareholder returns. While these measures remain important, they provide an incomplete picture in an era where startups, investors, and ecosystems face complex challenges that transcend financial boundaries. Today, success must also account for social impact, environmental sustainability, innovation capacity, and long-term resilience. Rethinking metrics of success is critical for building businesses that not only thrive economically but also contribute positively to society and the planet.

This chapter explores the limitations of conventional metrics, the importance of adopting a broader perspective on success, and the emerging frameworks that align business objectives with societal and environmental goals. Through case studies and actionable strategies, we examine how startups, investors, and ecosystems can redefine success to create lasting value.

The Limitations of Traditional Metrics

Overemphasis on Short-Term Financial Gains

Traditional metrics such as quarterly earnings and profit margins prioritize short-term performance, often at the expense of long-term sustainability. This approach can lead to:

- **Underinvestment in Innovation**: Companies focused on immediate financial returns may neglect research and development, stifling their ability to adapt and grow.
- **Erosion of Trust**: Prioritizing profits over stakeholders' well-being can damage relationships with employees, customers, and communities.

- **Environmental and Social Neglect**: A narrow focus on financial metrics often overlooks the broader impact of business operations on society and the environment.

Ignoring Intangible Assets

Traditional metrics often fail to capture the value of intangible assets such as intellectual property, brand reputation, and human capital. These assets are increasingly critical in a knowledge-driven economy and play a significant role in determining long-term success.

Misalignment with Societal Goals

Businesses that focus solely on financial performance may miss opportunities to address pressing societal challenges. For example, a company that prioritizes cost-cutting over environmental responsibility might contribute to climate change, undermining its long-term viability and reputation.

The Case for Broader Metrics of Success

Aligning Business Goals with Societal Impact

Broadening the definition of success allows businesses to align their objectives with societal needs, creating value that extends beyond shareholders to include employees, customers, communities, and the environment. This alignment enhances trust, loyalty, and long-term resilience.

Driving Innovation and Resilience

Metrics that prioritize long-term impact encourage investments in innovation, talent development, and sustainable practices. By fostering a culture of continuous improvement, businesses can adapt to changing market conditions and remain competitive.

Enhancing Stakeholder Relationships

Redefining success strengthens relationships with stakeholders by demonstrating a commitment to shared values. For example, companies that prioritize employee well-being often enjoy higher retention rates, greater productivity, and a more engaged workforce.

Emerging Frameworks for Measuring Success

Environmental, Social, and Governance (ESG) Metrics

ESG metrics evaluate a company's performance in areas such as environmental sustainability, social responsibility, and corporate governance. Examples include:

- **Environmental**: Carbon footprint, energy efficiency, and resource conservation.
- **Social**: Diversity and inclusion, employee satisfaction, and community engagement.
- **Governance**: Board diversity, ethical practices, and transparency.

ESG metrics provide a holistic view of a company's impact and are increasingly used by investors to assess long-term value.

Triple Bottom Line (TBL)

The TBL framework expands the traditional bottom line to include social and environmental considerations alongside financial performance. The three pillars of TBL are:

1. **Profit**: Financial sustainability and growth.
2. **People**: Social equity and well-being.
3. **Planet**: Environmental stewardship and sustainability.

By balancing these dimensions, businesses can achieve sustainable success that benefits all stakeholders.

Impact Measurement and Management (IMM)

IMM frameworks focus on measuring and managing the positive and negative impacts of a business's activities. Key components include:

- **Theory of Change**: Defining the intended outcomes and the steps needed to achieve them.
- **Impact Metrics**: Quantifying outcomes using indicators such as lives improved, emissions reduced, or jobs created.
- **Stakeholder Engagement**: Involving stakeholders in the design and evaluation of impact initiatives.

Integrated Reporting

Integrated reporting combines financial and non-financial information to provide a comprehensive view of a company's performance and strategy. This approach highlights how a company creates value over time, considering factors such as sustainability, innovation, and stakeholder relationships.

Strategies for Redefining Success

1. Setting Purpose-Driven Goals

Businesses should define success in terms of their broader purpose, aligning their goals with societal and environmental priorities. For example:

- A renewable energy startup might measure success by the amount of carbon emissions avoided.
- A healthcare company might focus on improving patient outcomes and access to care.

Purpose-driven goals inspire employees, attract customers, and differentiate businesses in competitive markets.

2. Engaging Stakeholders

Redefining success requires input from a diverse range of stakeholders, including employees, customers, investors, and communities. Engaging stakeholders ensures that metrics reflect shared values and priorities, fostering trust and collaboration.

3. Building Transparent and Accountable Systems

Transparency and accountability are essential for implementing broader metrics of success. Businesses should:

- Regularly report on their progress toward non-financial goals.
- Use third-party audits to validate their impact.
- Communicate openly about challenges and opportunities.

4. Leveraging Technology for Measurement

Advances in technology enable more accurate and efficient measurement of success metrics. For example:

- **Data Analytics**: Tools for analyzing large datasets to track progress and identify trends.
- **Blockchain**: Secure and transparent record-keeping for supply chain sustainability.
- **AI and Machine Learning**: Predictive models for assessing the long-term impact of business decisions.

5. Fostering a Culture of Innovation and Responsibility

Redefining success requires a cultural shift within organizations. Leaders must:

- Champion the importance of non-financial metrics.

- Empower employees to innovate and take ownership of impact initiatives.
- Celebrate successes and learn from failures.

Case Studies: Businesses Redefining Success

1. Patagonia

Patagonia's commitment to environmental sustainability is a cornerstone of its success. The company measures impact through initiatives such as recycled materials, carbon neutrality goals, and support for environmental activism. By prioritizing purpose alongside profit, Patagonia has built a loyal customer base and a strong brand.

2. Unilever

Unilever's Sustainable Living Plan integrates social and environmental goals into its business strategy. Metrics such as reducing greenhouse gas emissions, improving health and well-being, and enhancing livelihoods demonstrate the company's holistic approach to success.

3. Tesla

Tesla's mission to accelerate the transition to sustainable energy drives its innovation and growth. Success metrics include the number of electric vehicles sold, the expansion of renewable energy infrastructure, and reductions in greenhouse gas emissions.

The Role of Investors and Ecosystems

Encouraging Long-Term Thinking

Investors play a critical role in redefining success by prioritizing long-term value creation over short-term gains. Impact investing,

ESG integration, and shareholder advocacy are strategies that align investment decisions with broader metrics of success.

Supporting Ecosystem Collaboration

Innovation ecosystems can facilitate the adoption of broader success metrics by fostering collaboration, sharing best practices, and providing resources. For example:

- Accelerators and incubators can mentor startups in impact measurement.
- Industry coalitions can develop standardized frameworks for ESG reporting.
- Governments can create incentives for businesses that prioritize social and environmental goals.

The Broader Implications of Rethinking Success

Redefining metrics of success has profound implications for businesses, society, and the planet. By embracing a holistic approach, we can:

- Drive meaningful progress on global challenges such as climate change, inequality, and public health.
- Foster trust and collaboration among stakeholders.
- Build resilient businesses that thrive in an uncertain and rapidly changing world.

Conclusion

Rethinking metrics of success is no longer an option but a necessity in today's interconnected and dynamic world. By expanding the definition of success to include social impact, environmental sustainability, and long-term resilience, businesses can create value that benefits all stakeholders. Through purpose-driven goals, stakeholder engagement, and innovative measurement frameworks, startups, investors, and ecosystems can lead the way in building a more equitable and sustainable future.

As we redefine what it means to succeed, we unlock the potential for innovation that not only drives economic growth but also addresses the most pressing challenges of our time.

Chapter 11: Building for Sustainability

Sustainability has become a cornerstone of modern innovation and business strategy, driven by growing awareness of environmental, social, and economic challenges. Building for sustainability involves creating systems, products, and organizations that meet present needs without compromising the ability of future generations to meet theirs. This chapter explores the principles, practices, and strategies essential for integrating sustainability into startups, ecosystems, and innovation efforts.

The Urgency of Sustainability

Environmental Imperatives

Global challenges such as climate change, resource depletion, and biodiversity loss underscore the urgent need for sustainable practices. Key drivers include:

- **Carbon Emissions**: Rising greenhouse gas emissions threaten ecosystems, economies, and communities.
- **Resource Scarcity**: Overconsumption of finite resources creates vulnerabilities in supply chains and markets.
- **Pollution**: Waste and pollution from industrial processes harm human health and the environment.

Social Considerations

Sustainability also addresses social inequities, aiming to create inclusive systems that promote well-being for all. This includes:

- **Equity and Inclusion**: Addressing disparities in access to resources, opportunities, and decision-making.
- **Community Resilience**: Strengthening local capacities to adapt to environmental and economic shocks.

- **Health and Education**: Ensuring that basic needs are met for present and future generations.

Economic Drivers

Sustainability is not only an ethical imperative but also an economic opportunity. Businesses that adopt sustainable practices often gain competitive advantages, including:

- **Cost Savings**: Efficiency improvements reduce waste and resource consumption.
- **Market Access**: Growing consumer demand for sustainable products opens new revenue streams.
- **Risk Mitigation**: Sustainable practices help manage risks related to regulation, reputation, and resource scarcity.

Principles of Sustainable Innovation

Systems Thinking

Sustainability requires a holistic approach that considers the interconnections between environmental, social, and economic factors. Systems thinking helps innovators identify leverage points and unintended consequences within complex systems.

Circularity

A circular economy replaces the traditional linear model of "take-make-waste" with a regenerative approach that minimizes waste and maximizes resource efficiency. Principles include:

- Designing for durability, repairability, and recyclability.
- Recovering and repurposing materials at the end of a product's life cycle.
- Using renewable resources wherever possible.

Resilience

Resilience focuses on building systems that can adapt to and recover from disruptions. This includes diversifying supply chains, decentralizing operations, and fostering innovation that anticipates future challenges.

Stakeholder Engagement

Sustainability is a collective effort that requires input and collaboration from diverse stakeholders. Engaging employees, customers, suppliers, and communities ensures that solutions are relevant, equitable, and effective.

Strategies for Sustainable Startups

1. Embedding Sustainability in the Business Model

Sustainability should be integrated into the core of a startup's business model rather than treated as an afterthought. This includes:

- Aligning products and services with environmental and social goals.
- Identifying opportunities for innovation that address sustainability challenges.
- Building metrics to measure impact alongside financial performance.

2. Prioritizing Resource Efficiency

Startups can reduce their environmental footprint and operational costs by optimizing resource use. Strategies include:

- Implementing energy-efficient technologies.
- Reducing material waste through better design and production processes.
- Leveraging data analytics to identify inefficiencies.

3. Leveraging Technology and Innovation

Technological advancements play a critical role in enabling sustainability. Examples include:

- **Clean Energy**: Developing renewable energy solutions and storage technologies.
- **Smart Systems**: Using IoT and AI to optimize energy, water, and resource consumption.
- **Biotechnology**: Creating sustainable alternatives to traditional materials and processes.

4. Building Partnerships

Collaboration with stakeholders amplifies the impact of sustainability initiatives. Partnerships can provide access to expertise, resources, and networks. Examples include:

- Working with suppliers to improve supply chain sustainability.
- Partnering with NGOs and governments on community development projects.
- Joining industry coalitions to set standards and share best practices.

5. Designing for Scalability

Sustainable solutions must be scalable to achieve widespread impact. Startups should:

- Focus on modular and adaptable designs that can grow with demand.
- Build infrastructure and processes that support long-term growth.
- Consider partnerships and funding strategies that enable scale.

The Role of Ecosystems in Supporting Sustainability

Creating Collaborative Platforms

Innovation ecosystems can facilitate collaboration between startups, corporations, researchers, and policymakers. Examples include:

- Green innovation hubs that provide funding, mentorship, and testing facilities for sustainable ventures.
- Knowledge-sharing platforms that disseminate best practices and case studies.
- Public-private partnerships that align efforts across sectors.

Providing Access to Resources

Ecosystems can support startups by providing access to critical resources, such as:

- Funding: Grants, impact investments, and green bonds incentivize sustainable practices.
- Talent: Training programs and networks connect startups with skilled professionals.
- Data: Open data initiatives enable startups to analyze trends and optimize solutions.

Advocating for Policy Support

Policy frameworks play a crucial role in enabling sustainability. Ecosystems can advocate for:

- Incentives such as tax breaks, subsidies, and grants for sustainable businesses.
- Standards and certifications that promote accountability and transparency.
- Regulatory reforms that remove barriers to innovation and adoption.

Measuring and Communicating Impact

Defining Metrics

Measuring sustainability impact requires clear and relevant metrics. Common frameworks include:

- **Carbon Footprint**: Measuring greenhouse gas emissions across operations and supply chains.
- **Circularity Indicators**: Tracking material reuse, recycling rates, and waste reduction.
- **Social Metrics**: Assessing community benefits, employee well-being, and equitable access.

Transparent Reporting

Transparency builds trust and accountability. Startups should:

- Publish regular sustainability reports that detail progress and challenges.
- Use standardized frameworks such as the Global Reporting Initiative (GRI) or Sustainability Accounting Standards Board (SASB).
- Engage stakeholders in the reporting process to ensure relevance and inclusivity.

Storytelling and Branding

Effective communication helps startups build support for their sustainability initiatives. Strategies include:

- Highlighting the positive impact of products and practices.
- Sharing success stories and testimonials from customers and partners.
- Using branding and marketing to align with sustainability values.

Case Studies: Startups Leading in Sustainability

1. Beyond Meat

Beyond Meat has redefined the food industry by offering plant-based alternatives to meat. The company's innovations reduce greenhouse gas emissions, water use, and deforestation compared to traditional animal agriculture.

2. Fairphone

Fairphone designs modular smartphones with a focus on ethical sourcing, durability, and repairability. Its approach promotes circularity and reduces electronic waste.

3. BioLite

BioLite creates energy solutions for off-grid communities, combining clean cooking stoves with solar lighting and charging systems. The company addresses energy access and reduces indoor air pollution.

The Future of Sustainability in Innovation

Embracing Regenerative Design

The next frontier in sustainability is regenerative design, which goes beyond minimizing harm to actively restoring ecosystems and communities. Examples include:

- Regenerative agriculture practices that enhance soil health and biodiversity.
- Urban planning initiatives that create green spaces and improve air quality.
- Technologies that capture and repurpose carbon emissions.

Leveraging Emerging Technologies

Advances in areas such as blockchain, quantum computing, and synthetic biology offer new opportunities to address sustainability challenges. For example:

- Blockchain can enhance supply chain transparency and traceability.
- Quantum computing can optimize energy systems and accelerate material discovery.
- Synthetic biology can create bio-based materials and processes.

Fostering a Global Movement

Sustainability is a global challenge that requires collective action. Startups, ecosystems, governments, and communities must work together to:

- Set ambitious goals aligned with global frameworks such as the UN Sustainable Development Goals (SDGs).
- Share knowledge and resources across borders.
- Inspire cultural shifts toward sustainable consumption and production.

Conclusion

Building for sustainability is not just a moral imperative; it is a strategic advantage that drives innovation, resilience, and long-term value. By integrating sustainability into business models, fostering collaboration, and embracing emerging technologies, startups and ecosystems can create solutions that address global challenges and build a better future.

As the world moves toward a more sustainable paradigm, the ability to innovate responsibly and inclusively will define the leaders of tomorrow. By prioritizing sustainability today, we lay the foundation for a thriving and equitable world for generations to come.

Chapter 12: The Vision Ahead

As we stand at the intersection of rapid technological change and unprecedented global challenges, the future of innovation holds immense promise. Startups, ecosystems, and investors have the power to shape this future by embracing a vision that prioritizes collaboration, sustainability, and impact. The next generation of innovation must not only drive economic growth but also address societal challenges, empower communities, and create a more equitable and resilient world.

This chapter explores the elements of a forward-looking vision for innovation. It examines emerging trends, the role of technology, and the importance of inclusivity and ethics in shaping the future. By outlining actionable strategies, we aim to inspire startups and ecosystems to lead the way in building a better tomorrow.

The Future of Innovation: Key Trends

1. The Convergence of Technologies

The future will be defined by the convergence of multiple technologies, creating synergies that unlock new possibilities. Key areas include:

- **Artificial Intelligence and Quantum Computing**: AI will leverage quantum computing to solve complex problems, from drug discovery to climate modeling.
- **Biotechnology and Data Analytics**: Advances in genomics and big data will enable precision medicine and sustainable agriculture.
- **IoT and Blockchain**: The integration of IoT devices with blockchain technology will enhance transparency and security in supply chains, healthcare, and smart cities.

2. Decentralization and Democratization

Decentralization will empower individuals and communities by distributing power and resources. Examples include:

- **Decentralized Finance (DeFi)**: Blockchain-based financial systems that provide access to banking services without intermediaries.
- **Distributed Energy Systems**: Renewable energy microgrids that enable local generation and consumption.
- **Open Innovation**: Collaborative models that leverage crowd-sourced knowledge and resources.

3. The Rise of Regenerative Practices

Regenerative practices will move beyond sustainability to actively restore ecosystems and communities. Innovations will focus on:

- **Circular Economies**: Designing systems that eliminate waste and regenerate natural resources.
- **Regenerative Agriculture**: Farming practices that restore soil health and biodiversity.
- **Green Infrastructure**: Urban designs that integrate natural ecosystems to improve resilience and quality of life.

4. The Human-Centered Approach

Technology will increasingly focus on enhancing human well-being and fostering meaningful connections. This includes:

- **Mental Health Technologies**: AI-driven tools for early diagnosis and personalized treatment.
- **Inclusive Design**: Products and services that cater to diverse populations, including those with disabilities.
- **Educational Innovation**: Adaptive learning platforms that empower individuals to thrive in a knowledge-driven economy.

The Role of Technology in Shaping the Future

Enabling Large-Scale Impact

Technology has the potential to address some of humanity's most pressing challenges. Examples include:

- **Climate Change Mitigation**: AI-powered analytics for optimizing renewable energy deployment and carbon capture technologies.
- **Global Health**: Genomic research and AI-driven diagnostics to combat pandemics and rare diseases.
- **Food Security**: Precision agriculture and lab-grown meat to ensure sustainable food production.

Enhancing Collaboration and Connectivity

Technological advancements will enable seamless collaboration across borders and disciplines. Tools such as virtual reality and AI-powered communication platforms will foster innovation by connecting diverse perspectives and expertise.

Empowering Individuals and Communities

Decentralized technologies will empower individuals and communities to take control of their resources, data, and decision-making processes. This shift will democratize innovation and create opportunities for grassroots solutions.

Inclusivity and Ethics in Innovation

Bridging the Digital Divide

Ensuring equitable access to technology is critical for creating an inclusive future. Strategies include:

- Expanding broadband infrastructure to underserved regions.
- Developing affordable and accessible devices.
- Providing digital literacy programs to empower marginalized communities.

Ethical Frameworks for Innovation

As technology becomes increasingly pervasive, ethical considerations must guide its development and use. This includes:

- **Data Privacy and Security**: Protecting individuals' data and preventing misuse.
- **Bias and Fairness**: Ensuring AI algorithms and decision-making systems are free from bias.
- **Sustainability**: Minimizing the environmental impact of technology production and use.

Empowering Diverse Voices

Diversity in innovation leads to more creative and impactful solutions. Startups and ecosystems should prioritize:

- **Inclusive Hiring**: Building teams that reflect diverse perspectives and experiences.
- **Community Engagement**: Involving local stakeholders in the design and implementation of solutions.
- **Representation in Leadership**: Ensuring diversity in decision-making roles within organizations.

Strategies for Building the Future

1. Cultivating a Culture of Experimentation

Innovation thrives in environments that encourage experimentation and learning from failure. Strategies include:

- **Lean Methodologies**: Rapid prototyping and iterative development to refine ideas.
- **Safe Spaces for Testing**: Creating regulatory sandboxes and pilot programs to explore new concepts.
- **Celebrating Failures**: Viewing setbacks as opportunities for growth and learning.

2. Strengthening Ecosystem Collaboration

Collaboration between startups, corporations, governments, and academia will amplify the impact of innovation. Ecosystems should:

- Facilitate cross-sector partnerships and knowledge sharing.
- Provide platforms for networking and collaboration.
- Align efforts with global goals such as the UN Sustainable Development Goals (SDGs).

3. Investing in Talent and Education

Developing the next generation of innovators requires investments in talent and education. This includes:

- Supporting STEM education and lifelong learning initiatives.
- Offering mentorship and training programs for entrepreneurs.
- Encouraging interdisciplinary approaches that combine technical and creative skills.

4. Leveraging Emerging Technologies

Startups and ecosystems must stay ahead of technological trends by:

- Exploring applications of AI, blockchain, and other emerging technologies.
- Building adaptability into systems to accommodate future advancements.
- Partnering with research institutions to translate breakthroughs into practical solutions.

The Vision of a Resilient and Equitable Future

Resilience in Uncertainty

The future will bring both opportunities and disruptions. Building resilience requires:

- Diversifying supply chains and revenue streams.
- Investing in adaptive infrastructure and systems.
- Fostering a culture of agility and continuous improvement.

Equity as a Guiding Principle

An equitable future ensures that the benefits of innovation are shared by all. Startups and ecosystems must:

- Address systemic inequalities in access to resources and opportunities.
- Design solutions that prioritize the needs of underserved populations.
- Advocate for policies that promote fairness and inclusion.

Creating a Legacy of Impact

Ultimately, the vision for the future of innovation is one of lasting impact. By addressing global challenges, empowering individuals, and fostering collaboration, we can build a world that is:

- Environmentally sustainable.
- Economically prosperous.
- Socially inclusive and just.

Conclusion

The vision ahead for innovation is one of boundless possibility. By embracing technological convergence, inclusivity, ethics, and sustainability, startups and ecosystems can lead the way in shaping a better future. Through collaboration, creativity, and a commitment to addressing humanity's most pressing challenges, we can unlock the full potential of innovation to create a world that is resilient, equitable, and thriving for generations to come.

The journey will not be without its challenges, but with a clear vision and a shared commitment to progress, the future is bright. Let us work together to turn this vision into reality, one innovation at a time.

Conclusion: Innovating for a Better Tomorrow

The world is at a critical juncture, marked by rapid technological advancements, mounting global challenges, and an unprecedented capacity for innovation. The decisions we make today as entrepreneurs, investors, and ecosystem builders will determine the trajectory of the future. As we look ahead, the imperative to innovate responsibly, inclusively, and sustainably has never been greater.

This essay delves into the overarching themes that define the innovation landscape of tomorrow. By reflecting on the lessons of the past, embracing the opportunities of the present, and envisioning the possibilities of the future, we can chart a path toward a world where innovation drives progress for all.

Reflecting on the Past: Lessons Learned

The Transformative Power of Technology

Throughout history, technological advancements have been the driving force behind societal progress. From the invention of the printing press to the digital revolution, innovation has reshaped how we live, work, and connect. These milestones demonstrate that technology can be a catalyst for economic growth, cultural enrichment, and improved quality of life.

However, the past also offers cautionary tales. Rapid industrialization brought unprecedented economic prosperity but also environmental degradation. The digital era has connected billions of people but has also raised concerns about privacy, misinformation, and social divides. These experiences underscore the importance of aligning innovation with ethical considerations and long-term goals.

The Role of Collaboration

No innovation exists in isolation. The most transformative breakthroughs—whether in healthcare, energy, or communication—have emerged from collaboration across disciplines, industries, and borders. The Human Genome Project, for example, succeeded because of the collective efforts of scientists, governments, and private entities worldwide.

Collaboration amplifies resources, fosters diverse perspectives, and accelerates problem-solving. Reflecting on the successes and challenges of past partnerships reveals the need to prioritize trust, transparency, and shared vision in future endeavors.

Embracing the Present: Opportunities and Challenges

A World of Accelerating Change

The pace of innovation today is unprecedented. Technologies such as artificial intelligence, biotechnology, and quantum computing are evolving at exponential rates, opening new frontiers in science, medicine, and industry. At the same time, global challenges such as climate change, inequality, and health crises demand urgent and coordinated action.

This dual reality—a world of boundless potential and pressing challenges—creates both opportunities and responsibilities. Innovators must harness the power of technology not only to create economic value but also to address systemic issues that affect communities and ecosystems worldwide.

The Importance of Inclusivity

Inclusivity is essential for meaningful innovation. Marginalized communities often face the greatest challenges but are frequently excluded from decision-making processes. By involving diverse voices in innovation, we can ensure that solutions are equitable, culturally relevant, and widely accessible.

Startups and ecosystems have a unique role to play in fostering inclusivity. From hiring practices that prioritize diversity to designing products that serve underrepresented groups, innovation can be a powerful force for social equity.

Ethical Innovation in a Digital Age

As digital technologies become increasingly pervasive, ethical considerations must guide their development and application. Issues such as data privacy, algorithmic bias, and the environmental impact of digital infrastructure require proactive solutions. Innovators must balance the pursuit of progress with the protection of individual rights and societal well-being.

Envisioning the Future: A Vision of Progress

The Convergence of Technology and Humanity

The future of innovation lies at the intersection of technology and humanity. Advances in artificial intelligence, robotics, and biotechnology have the potential to enhance human capabilities, extend life expectancy, and solve complex problems. However, realizing this potential requires a human-centered approach that prioritizes empathy, ethics, and inclusivity.

For example, AI-powered healthcare systems can improve diagnostics and treatment plans, but they must be designed to ensure fairness and accessibility. Similarly, autonomous vehicles promise safer and more efficient transportation, but their development must address regulatory, ethical, and infrastructural challenges.

Building Resilient Ecosystems

Resilience will be a defining characteristic of successful innovation ecosystems. In a world of rapid change and uncertainty, ecosystems must adapt to evolving technologies, market dynamics, and societal needs. This requires:

- **Collaboration**: Strengthening partnerships between startups, corporations, governments, and academia.
- **Sustainability**: Prioritizing environmental stewardship and resource efficiency.
- **Flexibility**: Creating systems that can pivot and scale in response to new challenges and opportunities.

Empowering the Next Generation

The future belongs to the next generation of innovators. By investing in education, mentorship, and capacity-building, we can equip young leaders with the skills and mindset needed to tackle tomorrow's challenges. This includes:

- Encouraging interdisciplinary approaches that combine technical expertise with creative problem-solving.
- Providing access to resources and networks that support entrepreneurial endeavors.
- Cultivating a sense of purpose and responsibility in addressing global issues.

The Call to Action

For Entrepreneurs

Entrepreneurs are at the forefront of innovation. By embracing a problem-solving mindset and prioritizing impact, startups can create solutions that drive meaningful change. This requires:

- Aligning business models with social and environmental goals.
- Leveraging technology to address systemic challenges.
- Building inclusive and collaborative teams that reflect diverse perspectives.

For Investors

Investors have the power to shape the future by directing capital toward ventures that align with long-term value creation. This includes:

- Supporting startups that prioritize sustainability and equity.
- Advocating for metrics that go beyond financial returns to include impact and resilience.
- Fostering partnerships that amplify the reach and effectiveness of innovative solutions.

For Ecosystems

Innovation ecosystems must serve as enablers of progress. By fostering collaboration, providing resources, and promoting shared goals, ecosystems can drive transformative change. This involves:

- Creating platforms for cross-sector collaboration and knowledge exchange.
- Advocating for policies that support sustainable and inclusive innovation.
- Celebrating successes and learning from failures to build a culture of continuous improvement.

A Legacy of Innovation

The true measure of success in innovation is not just the products we create or the profits we generate but the legacy we leave behind. By prioritizing collaboration, inclusivity, and sustainability, we can build a world where innovation serves as a force for good.

As we look to the future, let us embrace the challenges and opportunities before us with courage, creativity, and a commitment to progress. Together, we can unlock the full potential of innovation to create a brighter, more equitable, and resilient tomorrow.

www.ingramcontent.com/pod-product-compliance
Lightning Source LLC
Chambersburg PA
CBHW062109220526
45471CB00010B/3670